Between Ignorance and Enlightenment (I)

By
Venerable Master Hsing Yun

Translated by
Ven. Miao Hsi and Cherry Lai

© 2002 Buddha's Light Publishing

By Venerable Master Hsing Yun
Translated by Venerable Miao Hsi and Cherry Lai
Edited by Robin Stevens and Brenda Bolinger
Proofread by Dr. Tom Manzo
Book and cover designed by Mei-Chi Shih

Published by Buddha's Light Publishing
3456 S. Glenmark Drive,
Hacienda Heights, CA 91745, U.S.A.
Tel: (626) 923-5143 / (626) 961-9697
Fax: (626) 923-5145 / (626) 369-1944
e-mail: itc@blia.org

Protected by copyright under the terms of the International Copyright Union; all rights reserved. Except for fair use in book reviews, no part of this book may be reproduced for any reason by any means, including any method of photographic reproduction, without permission of the publisher. Printed in Taiwan.

ISBN: 0-9715612-0-6
Library of Congress Control Number: 2001099611

~ Table of Contents ~

Foreword -- i
Introduction ------------------------------------ iii
Words from the Editor --------------------------- vii

The Beauty of Being Natural 1

To Think Positively 3

Even the Inanimate Teaches the Dharma 6

The Value of Travel 8

To Live is to Move 10

Understanding Time 12

Wonderful Deeds and Toughing Stories 14

Provide Others with Good Causes and Conditions 16

The Value of Giving 18

A Good Sense of Humor 20

Take Delight in Shared Joy 22

The Beauty in Magnanimity 24

The Way to Happiness 27

Creating Positive and Uplifting Knowledge 29

The Importance of Being a Law-abiding Citizen 31

Where is Justice? 33

Illicit Possession 35

A Gilded Dinner Table 37

How to Change Fate 39

All in a Thought 41

Overcoming Fear 43

Ridding Ourselves of Stress 45

Beauty and Ugliness 47

The Unsurpassed Value of Impermanence 49

Between Success and Failure 51

A Carefree Life 53

The True Meaning of Love 55

The Value of Perception 57

Have Respect for Life 59

To Live in Peace and Quiet 62

Establish Yourself 65

Live Courageously 67

The Significance of Breathing 69

The Strength of Commitment 71

Strive for Progress Against All Odds 73

To Be Unfettered by Worry and Joy 74

To Live in Hope 76

Walk with Right Path 78

Where There is Dharma, There is a Way 80

A Moment of Awakening 82

Freedom from Fear 84

To Forbear a Moment's Anger 87

To Purposely Confuse the Bad and the Good	89
To Have Resolve and Make Vows	91
The Truth is the Path	93
The Value of Truth	95
The Meaning of Compassion	97
Follow the Circumstances	99
Levels of Faith	101
True Equality	104
To Reform Oneself	106
Patience and Persistence	108
Humility and Shame	110
Vanity and Practicality	112
Having and Using	114
Begin from the Self	116
Be Optimistic and Progressive	118
Twelve Questions for Introspection	120
The Definition of Success	123
Trust and Reputation	125
Glossary	127

Acknowledgements

We received a lot of help from many people and we want to thank them for their efforts in making the publication of this book possible. We especially appreciate Venerable Tzu Jung, the Chief Executive of Fo Guang Shan International Translation Center (F.G.S.I.T.C.), Venerable Hui Chuan, the Abbot of Hsi Lai Temple, and Venerable Yi Chao, the Director of F.G.S.I.T.C. for their support and leadership; Venerable Miao Hsi and Cherry Lai for their translation; Robin Stevens and Brenda Bolinger for their editing; Dr. Tom Manzo for his proofreading; Mei-Chi Shih for her book and cover design; Venerable Miao Han, Mae Chu, Mu-Tzen Hsu, Ching Tay, Echo Tsai, and Oscar Mauricio for preparing the manuscript for publication. Our appreciation also goes to everyone who has supported this project from its conception to its completion.

BETWEEN IGNORANCE AND ENLIGHTENMENT

FOREWORD

Since the inauguration of the daily paper, *The Merit Times* in Taiwan on April 1, 2001, I have been writing an article each day for the column "Between Ignorance and Enlightenment." It has now been more than a year and a half and I am still writing.

In the beginning, I was only trying it out, thinking I would finish in a couple of months. However, response from readers has been very enthusiastic, and I just could not stop writing.

Among the feedback from our readers, the staff at *The Merit Times* reported that many people subscribed to the paper because they wanted to read "Between Ignorance and Enlightenment." Some readers also indicated that after reading the column, their interests and skills in writing have improved. With their polished writing skills they were even able to gain acceptance to a university. Other readers made scrapbooks of the articles and used them as bedtime reading.

In addition, some people who previously had numerous unwholesome habits have changed for the better after reading the column. For instance, they have quit smoking, drinking, and gambling. There were also cases where family members had problems getting along with each other and they were inspired by the articles. Their families have become harmonious and joyful, filled with laughter and warmth. Some students wrote reports based on the articles and obtained high grades and commendation from their teachers.

These responses from different walks of life greatly reinforced my sense of duty for the column. Because of this mission, which I feel I must shoulder myself, I am motivated to write each and every day, regardless of how busy my schedule may be in propagating the Dharma. I can always find time during the day to make connections with the readers through my writing.

The English section of the American edition of *The Merit Times* is also publishing the articles translated by Hsi Lai Temple. Many study groups organized by members of the Buddha's Light International Association are using the articles for their discussions. Numerous readers have since called for a collective publication of these articles and their earnest requests are now fulfilled.

The meaning of *Between Ignorance and Enlightenment* is actually reflected in our everyday life, where there are inevitably many situations involving both "ignorance" and "enlightenment." Sometimes, those directly affected are deluded, while those around them may see through the situation very clearly. Therefore, a few appropriate words will be of much help in pointing the way to a breakthrough, providing food for thought at the same time.

In reality, ignorance and enlightenment lie in just a thought! A thought of ignorance may cause sorrow and pain while an inspiration of enlightenment can bring out the sun of wisdom. Just as Buddhist sutras indicate, "Troubles are Bodhi, and Bodhi is trouble!" The sourness of pineapples and grapes can be turned into sweetness with sunshine and warm breezes. Therefore, by being able to reflect and contemplate on the sourness of our ignorance, we can taste the sweetness of enlightenment right here and now.

This short publication is the first of a series of an estimated ten volumes. Through *Between Ignorance and Enlightenment*, I wish to share and grow with all my readers!

Hsing Yun

INTRODUCTION

The opening lines of Charles Dickens' *A Tale of Two Cities* are well known for their paradoxical profundity, touting the setting of the novel as simultaneously "the best of times . . . the worst of times, the age of wisdom. . . the age of foolishness, the epoch of belief . . . the epoch of incredulity," pairing light and darkness, hope and despair, heaven and hell. The message seems to be that the human condition routinely sets us between these extremes of expectations and fears, that life is a double-edged sword to be wielded wisely and with great care. Or, as Master Hsing Yun succinctly observes: "Everything is within our own mind." This does not mean that the world is a mere projection of the mind, but rather that we are endlessly interpreting, conflating, and distorting the bare facts of experience through the narrow lenses of our isolated existence. As a result, we fail to truly see what is right before our eyes.

Being a skilled Buddhist Master, Master Hsing Yun is not content simply to set forth his astute observation about the mind. Rather, he makes this the starting point for a multi-dimensional tour of the pitfalls and potentials inherent within the confines of human life. Once we realize, as did Shakespeare's *Hamlet*, that "there is nothing either good or bad, but thinking makes it so," it becomes a matter of changing our thinking (to which Buddhism adds speech and behavior) in order to affect changes in our perceived reality.

Hidden within the sweeping technological advances and unprecedented prosperity we pride ourselves on, lie the seeds of anxiety, anger, fear and self-destruction. To counter these adverse effects, Master Hsing Yun launches us on a wide-ranging voyage of personal discovery offering insights on topics as diverse as time management and magnanimity, stress and the power of positive thinking, the value of impermanence and true love. There is much practical wisdom contained in these pages, set forth in easily digested tidbits that allow the reader to sample the smorgasbord at will. It is a wisdom firmly grounded in Buddhist philosophy, with its more than twenty-five centuries of careful evaluations of the human condition. These insights are vivid and provocative, challenging us to step back from our conditioned responses to life to see things as they really are. For example, travel is lauded as outdoor education, which can lead to inner awakening. Our obsession to stay tuned to unfolding events is contrasted by the advantages of uplifting news as positive reinforcement. Compassion is lauded over pity, forgiveness over lingering resentment. We are encouraged to question the unexamined stereotypes of what insures happiness, money, fame, success, and even love. The joy of non-attachment is heartily recommended in place of these egotistical dead-ends.

  In a world seemingly devoid of moral values, Master Hsing Yun calls upon us to renew our commitment to citizenship in the interest of social order and seek out justice beneath the superficial semblance of a society that ascribes to survival of the fittest. Wisdom is the antidote to fear, in all its forms. Perhaps most surprising of all, impermanence is exalted as an "unsurpassed value", given its power of change as infinite transformation, negative to positive as well as positive to negative. This same wisdom allows us to let go of stress, while opening "our heart as wide as the ocean." Our comfortable assumptions about life must be radically reconsidered, as we look beyond short-term effects to place our experience in perspective. A carefree life in the deepest sense requires equanimity and magnanimity, which in turn presupposes the ability to liberate ourselves from all bonds and dependencies.

"True love is not a possession; it is a sacrifice", Master Hsing Yun declares, which very few are ready to undertake in today's world. Such love is closely aligned with the forces of Truth, Justice, and Goodness. Life must be respected in all its forms, including the environment, due to the fact of mutual dependency. Courage and commitment, progress and hope, are but a few of the components of a meaningful life touched upon. Peace and quiet are to be found not in some external locale, but rather discovered within.

To uncover that peace, Master Hsing Yun encourages us to take responsibility for ourselves, to practice forbearance, patience, and persistence; experience humility, shame, and regret for our mistakes; and fuel our resolve to improve with vows. As Master Hsing Yun asks us to re-examine our definitions of success and failure, wealth and poverty, he offers us new ways to fully understand the world and our role in it; compassion comes from kindness, truth from clarity, and the beauty of human nature from a moment of awakening.

For those willing to seriously contemplate the inner treasures and potentials discussed by Master Hsing Yun in this volume, what appears to be the "worst of times may yet be transmuted into the best of times", in which wisdom supplants foolishness and belief replaces incredulity. There is no better place to begin the "Twelve Questions for Introspection" provided in the text, salutary guidelines for self-help in any age. The pervasive tone of optimism gives good reason for hope to all who peruse these pages.

Sandra A. Wawrytko, Ph.D.
Departments of Asian Studies and Philosophy
San Diego State University
February 23, 2001

Words from the Editor

We own the whole universe in our minds and embrace endless realms in our hearts.

As we traverse the ups and downs of daily living in this modern world, we often find ourselves in need of inspiration and motivation. Rapid technological changes have created social upheavals in family structure and the way in which we live, creating stress in our lives that can often feel unbearable. We ask ourselves: how do we lead good, fulfilling lives? How do we face the constant barrage of violence and negativity in the media? How do we integrate spirituality into the fabric of our lives? As the quote above suggests, and as Buddhism teaches, the answers to these questions lie within each and every one of us.

First published in a daily column of *The Merit Times* newspaper, the articles in this collection were written by Venerable Master Hsing Yun, the charismatic founder of Fo Guang Shan Buddhist Order and the 48th Patriarch of the Linji (Rinzai) Chan School of Buddhism. Fo Guang Shan has grown from its roots as a small temple in Taiwan to one of the largest international Buddhist organizations in the world with branches worldwide. Venerable Master Hsing Yun writes prolifically on Buddhist sutras and a wide spectrum of topics, spreading the Dharma, the teachings of Buddhism, to people everywhere. This work represents yet another effort to plant the seeds of Humanistic Buddhism in the path of every person, to bridge the gap between East and West, and to enhance interfaith understanding and tolerance. Dedicating his life to this cause, his writings are motivational and inspirational.

Written in Chinese and then translated and published in

English, the short vignettes in this compilation are intended to instruct, motivate, inspire, and guide readers on their journey to spiritual discovery. They provide laypeople with introductory readings about the core teachings of Buddhism, teachings that can be applied to everyday living. The book can be read all at once or the articles read one at a time. Given the busy and hectic schedules of modern life, the length of the articles lend themselves to quick and easy reading, yet they can be contemplated for hours.

Through an examination of historical and current events, the articles in this book contextualize the basic teachings of Buddhism in the present, guiding us to open our minds and to practice compassion, magnanimity, and forbearance toward others. Using anecdotal evidence and examples from world and Buddhist history, we learn how Buddhist thinking can be applied to past events and continue to be relevant in the present as we confront modern problems, such as AIDS and the potential dangers of the internet. We learn to seek out stories of kindness and inspiration in the media instead of only listening to the negative ones. We learn that through our own thoughts and actions we can affect our karma and that of others when we give good causes and conditions to others by offering encouragement and taking joy in their accomplishments. We are taught that small steps count toward the whole and that by simply changing our thinking and sharing joy with others we can improve our own paths.

Between Ignorance and Enlightenment is a stepping stone to meditation and other Buddhist practice. It is hoped that in reading these articles, the door to inquiry and discovery will be opened permanently and the teachings of Buddhism will become an integral part of daily living.

Robin Stevens

The Beauty of Being Natural

We all pursue beauty. When we are not born with natural beauty, we turn to beauty products and even cosmetic surgery to enhance our looks. But no matter how hard we try to achieve the perfect look, it never compares to the beauty of just being natural.

Look at the beauty of nature: the crystal blue sky, the floating white clouds, the colorful hues of a rainbow after it rains, and the twinkling stars at night. Go climb to the top of a mountain at night, when the moon is bright and the air is crisp, and as far as the eye can see, you can appreciate the panoramic beauty of nature and the vast openness of the universe. In this universe of ours, there are lofty mountains and steep cliffs, there are boundless deserts, there are rushing rivers and lush forests. All these naturally beautiful landscapes of the world are odes of praise to the beauty and wonder of nature. The beauty of nature is really enchanting and fascinating!

In the pursuit of beauty, where it is lacking naturally we may make up for it artificially. Whether we are landscaping a garden, decorating a house, fashioning a wardrobe, or even changing our physical figure or posture, we need to harmonize these activities with nature in order to achieve a good standard of beauty. If buildings are ostentatiously designed or people overly made-up, they no longer reflect the beauty of

The beauty of nature is really enchanting and fascinating.

nature. Natural beauty is forfeited when we are pretentious or affected.

Although there seems to be no universal standard for beauty, there should be some guiding principles for it. Beauty should be pleasant to behold. It should purify one's spirit, sublimate one's mind, open up one's heart and transcend worldliness. The true meaning of beauty lies in its ability to enhance our lives.

In pursuing the beauty of being natural, we should speak with humor, we should be reasonable with others, and we should be gracious in how we handle world affairs. Then the beauty of being natural may be close at hand. The valor of men and the gentleness of women, the kindliness of seniors and the innocence of children are all life's examples of beauty in being natural.

To Think Positively

Humans are thinking animals! Since the beginning of time there have always been people who fantasize, who have delusions, who dream - and many who have ideals. When we lie in our beds at night, we should be free from worry. Yet thoughts about our lives often arise then; thoughts about family, our country, or even the world. Everything is within our mind.

One of the Buddhist sutras teaches us that humans are the combination of the five aggregates, another name for "I." The five aggregates are form, feelings, perception, mental formations, and consciousness. Perception or thinking is one of the five parts of the "I." Form and consciousness are our body and mind, respectively. Feelings is in both the body and mind. There are different kinds of feelings; feelings of suffering, enjoyment, or even neutral feelings. With conception, there can be kind, evil, or neutral thoughts. The average person often tends to think of himself or herself in a more positive light, but may have negative thoughts about others.

In our thoughts, when something concerns us, even if it is not good, we tend to be forgiving toward ourselves; but when something of a negative nature concerns others, we are less likely to be as forgiving. Humans tend to be forgiving toward the self and strict with others. However, if we are as critical of ourselves as we are of others, and as positive about and forgiving of others as we are about and of ourselves, then life will truly be wonderful.

The sutra says: "The three realms are all in the mind and all dharmas are in one's consciousness." In everyday life, we live in our delusions and with our thoughts create all sorts of fantasies out of nothing. Because it is impossible for humans to live without thoughts, we should make an effort to purify them. A pool of water needs to be purified before it is suitable for drinking. And when the stream of thinking is purified, it benefits both the self and others.

When we consider the thoughts of the saints and sages, we see that their thoughts are all about carrying the responsibilities of the world on their shoulders. But when we consider the thinking of those who are evil, we see that their thoughts are all about how to take advantage of others. In this world, there are so many people who wish to accommodate and help others; they sacrifice themselves for the good of humankind. However, there are many others who scheme and plot, with the intention of making trouble for others. A thought, then, could be heaven or could be hell.

When the stream of thinking is positive, it benefits both the self and others.

A thought could be about oneself, it could be about you, or it may be about him or her. We are all mixed together in one another's thoughts. There are thoughts about Buddhaland and the Pure Land. There are thoughts of gossip about others. Sometimes there are thoughts about evil spirits or animals. If all the abstract thoughts were to be accumulated together, the entire universe would not be large enough to contain so many troubling thoughts and delusions.

Since ancient times, questions about how to regard human thought have posed major problems to the world. Some believe that intellectuals should be respected. Although many great thinkers have been executed for their thoughts. Even so, they advocate freedom of thought. Thinking should indeed be free, but there should be guidelines for thought. A person who is able to think right, truthfully, kindly, beautifully, and positively about everything is truly wise.

Even the Inanimate Teaches the Dharma

We can divide the kaleidoscopic phenomena of the world into two different groups, sentient beings and the inanimate. Sentient beings are humans, birds, and animals, while the inanimate are mountains, rivers, trees, flowers and the like. When a sentient being teaches the Dharma, we can hear it; when the inanimate teaches, it is even more pleasant and moving to listen to. "When Master Daosheng speaks the Dharma, even the hard rock nods." You need not regard Master Daosheng as the only one who is teaching the Dharma; you may view the hard rock as the one doing the teaching. If the hard rock were not teaching, how could it nod?

We see white clouds floating freely in the sky and rivers meandering wistfully toward the sea; the ease of the white clouds and the wistfulness of the rivers tell us how carefree they are. We see the change of the seasons, the passing of time, the blooming and wilting of flowers, and the aging of life; these are nature's way of teaching us the meaning of impermanence.

We can use our ears to listen to the teachings of sentient beings, but we need to use our hearts to listen to the inanimate. Actually, everything in our daily lives is teaching us. The spring blossoms and autumn moon are pleasant to behold, and the singing birds and chirping bugs are delightful to hear. Even the tea of Chan Master Zhaozhou and the cookies of Chan Master Yunmen were used to teach the Dharma. Be it the sound of the temple drum, the ringing of the temple bell at dawn and dusk, or the symphony of the different Dharma instruments, all of these things teach us the Dharma.

Natural disasters are the earth's way of reminding us how

fragile our world is; wilting flowers are nature's way of teaching us about the impermanence of life. War and battles show us the suffering and emptiness of life; sickness, aging and death teach us that our body is the source of suffering. Look around you in your daily life. No matter whether you are getting dressed, taking a meal, resting or traveling about, or whether you are walking, waiting, sitting or sleeping, you see the arising, abiding, changing and extinction of all phenomena. We witness the birth, aging, sickness and death of sentient beings. These things all teach us the Dharma.

A Chan Master picked up a duster and said, "Do you understand?" If you understand the meaning of this, you are enlightened. A Chan Master may point to a tree in the garden and ask, "Do you know?" If you know, then you are a Chan practitioner. However, the echo of a deep valley or the music of nature is not so easily understood. "Eat when you are hungry and go to bed when you feel sleepy" is the Dharma of daily life. "To give without attachment and help others selflessly" is the highest form of teaching. If you can hear not only the teachings of sentient beings but also understand the teachings of the inanimate, then you have resolved the meaning of life. You can then rid yourself of ignorance and become enlightened.

Do the hard rocks have Buddha Nature?

The Value of Travel

Travel is very popular in modern society, which is beneficial for as the saying goes, "One should study ten thousand volumes of books and travel ten thousand miles of road." Not only can travel enrich our knowledge of geography, history, and culture, it can also provide an excellent opportunity to enjoy wonderful scenery and to enhance friendships with traveling companions.

Travel is a form of outdoor education because it is a means to expand one's view and world knowledge. It raises the quality of life and can promote business exchanges between countries. However, it is a shame that some people travel just for sensual pleasure; they travel to gamble or to seek physical thrills. Others indulge themselves with impulsive shopping, buying anything that appeals to them, thus winning themselves the notoriety of being a "shopping tourist." The purpose for travel should not be materialism but should instead be focused on intellectual cultivation and the enhancement of morals. For example, when parents travel with their children, the purpose of travel should not be based on vanity, but on learning at the same time the family is having fun. Families should take the opportunity to expand their views and knowledge, meeting people from diverse cultures, visiting historical sites and famous places, and making new friends. Furthermore, children should be taught to serve others, to develop their own thinking, to cultivate good manners, and to conduct themselves well in public.

Tourism is the smokeless industry of every country, and each country, without exception, should endeavor to develop their tourist industry. Under these circumstances the number of travel agents can proliferate; many people would be attracted by increased promotional efforts, organizing various tour groups to different and interesting places. However, there are some unethical travel agents who do not provide their customers with quality tours, but instead cheat and scheme to make a profit. In doing so, not only do they ruin their own reputations and spoil the vacations of the visitors, they also blemish the image of their country.

Life is short, so we should manage time wisely in order to do more to benefit society, maximizing every minute and hour. That is one way to improve the quality and use of our time. In addition, we should also explore and expand our vistas through learning more about other people in the world. Traveling helps us to live a quality life by opening our eyes to new things, developing our ties to other people and places, improving our knowledge, and learning good manners. It is indeed a good means to develop the value of life. Whenever we travel, we should go with the intention of learning; that way both our money and time are well spent.

After camping in the mountains and enduring the wilderness, we then realize the comfort of home. And if, after traveling for thousands of miles and taking in all the wonderful scenery, upon coming home we can realize our true nature - this is the meaning and value of travel.

To Live is To Move

We all engage our physical selves in motion or in movement. Those who are ill move less frequently or not at all; and in death we cease to move altogether. In nature, water needs to run freely in order to be clean, while air has to move in order to be fresh; similarly, as humans we need to be active to stay alive. The body and mind are constantly on the move: body, hands, heart, emotion, hearing, feeling, pulses, spirit, strength, action, and motive - sometimes even temper and anger. Therefore, the easiest way to cultivate oneself is to practice "beneficial movement" and to eliminate "bad movement." Beneficial movement harmonizes and purifies the body and mind.

Movement expresses energy and liveliness. According to the *Amitabha Sutra*, beings who lived in the Pure Land would daily "carry offerings of wondrous flowers to present to the Buddhas of the ten directions." In the *Diamond Sutra*, "The Buddha would put on his robe and carry his alms bowl to the city to beg for food. After the meal, he would practice walking meditation."

Avalokitesvara Bodhisattva "would manifest in thirty-two forms to deliver sentient beings." Ksitigarbha Bodhisattva vowed, "If I do not enter hell to save the beings there, who would?" All of these actions can be considered beneficial movement. Alone, Tang Dynasty's Venerable Master Xuanzang traversed eight hundred miles of desert on foot to get to India in order to bring Buddhist scriptures to China. Without this movement, Chinese culture and art would not be as rich as it is today. Columbus traveled thousands of miles across the ocean to explore the American continent; without this journey, the United States would not exist in the same form it does now.

Movement is the meaning and energy of life for, because of movement, we can progress and be active. Because of movement, we can learn with others and integrate into society, and thus gain the necessary support of others in what we do. A person's movements should not be judged alone, for we also need to look at the person and the event, as well as the action and the mind. If our speech has no benefit to others, then we should not speak; and if our thought has no benefit to others, then we should not think. If the steps we take have no benefit to others, then we should not proceed; and if the actions we make with our hands have no benefit to others, then we should not move. Therefore, we should only move when it is necessary, and only restrict our movement when it is not.

Self-cultivation is necessary for us to understand Buddhism. Similarly, in anything we do, practice is more important than theory, just as actions have more impact than mere empty words. People who know how to do things know how to make things come alive and develop their potential. People who know how to play chess know how to make their game come alive, and triumph over their opponent. People who know how to write know how to make their words come alive, and touch the hearts of others. People who know how to speak know how to make their speech come alive, and engage their audience.

Flowers bloom with all their fragrance while trees sway with the wind. We appreciate them because they are alive. Birds chirp in the trees, and we delight in their songs. Clouds gather and scatter in the sky, and we are relaxed by the peacefulness. Water in the brook cascades over the rocks, and we are refreshed by its coolness. We derive these positive feelings because all these movements are alive. To convey the hope and joy of life, then, we

Understanding Time

As we cross the threshold into the millennium, more and more people have begun to ponder the question of "time." According to reports, the United States has spent millions of dollars to build an eternal clock. It will only strike once every century, to remind people to slow down their steps and to reflect upon their shortcomings. To understand "time" and to successfully utilize "time" has indeed become a worthwhile issue for modern people.

Many people often complain about how time flies, while others complain about how time crawls. Some spend their time in search of fame and fortune instead of spending time with their loved ones, while others waste their time on trivial matters instead of using time to better themselves. If students are unwilling to spend time in the classroom, how can they acquire knowledge and broaden their horizons? If farmers are unwilling to spend time plowing their land, how can they reap a full harvest? It is clear that the way time is perceived is dependent upon how time is used.

Once upon a time, someone asked a Chan Master to teach him how to manage time. The Chan Master replied, "When time passes, it never returns; every second is thus precious." Hence, whoever can use time wisely has control of his or her life. It does not matter how old you are; what is important is how you manage your time.

"For a person who is exhausted, the road is long; for a person who cannot sleep, the night is endless; for a person who does not understand the truth, the reality of birth and death is far-reaching." We must understand that the past will never return, the present is gone in the blink of an eye, and the future is fast approaching and will become the past in no time. An eminent master of the past once said, "A day's time is more precious than the treasures of the universe."

As long as we can understand the fleeting essence of time and learn how to use time wisely, we can break the boundaries of time and transcend the limits of temporal space. As long as we can learn to treasure every second of our life and grasp every moment, we will be able to realize and experience the truth in the saying, "a moment is eternity." In this way, precious time is not limited to the tolling of the eternal clock.

It is important to know how to manage time wisely.

Wonderful Deeds and Touching Stories

"To overlook another's good deeds and publicize his wrongdoings" seems to be a common practice in today's society. It is a social disease that needs to be cured by praising one's virtues instead. Many wonderful things occur in society every day, events that are worthy of our attention. What we really need to do is to promote the good and to instill a sense of morality in a rapidly degrading world.

For example, recently Mr. Yang Fuyi miraculously wakened from a six-month coma caused by a massive brain hemorrhage. Although he has yet to recover his ability to communicate with words, and could initially only manage a smile or shake hands as a gesture of affection, speech therapy and other relevant care have been provided to him by the Creation of Life Foundation, a nonprofit organization, in the hope that he may one day regain the use of all his faculties.

In another example, Mrs. Bauer of New Mexico awoke from a long coma on Christmas Eve, 1999. She was comatose for sixteen years after giving birth to her fourth child. Her recovery has not only brought enormous joy to her children, but has also given much needed hope to families in similar situations.

During the earthquake in Taiwan, Baihao Temple was completely destroyed. In addition to being a place of worship for many Buddhists, it was a sanctuary for troubled youth. Recently, followers have organized a series of fundraising events for the purpose of collecting money to rebuild the temple. People from all walks of life have contributed to the cause.

Earlier this year, at the largest garden in suburban Taipei, sixty-four couples took their wedding vows in front of the Buddha.

Venerable Sheng-yen of Dharma Drum Buddhist Order presided over the unique ceremony, which brought a new aspect of Buddhism to the general public. In Taichung, more than 10,000 people joined Venerable Wei Chueh of Chung Tai Temple and Minister Wang Chinping of the Legislative Ministry of Taiwan in offering a candle of blessing to all living beings. The event was widely covered by the media and well received by the audience. When Tibetan monks were forced into exile in India by their own government, Indian authorities took extra measures to provide them with special care.

When Hu Yufan developed three of the world's smallest artificial satellites in the United States, he led humankind into a new frontier and brought unlimited benefits to the present and the future. When two whales were beached off the American coast last June, a group of caring scientists carefully nursed them back to health for their safe return to the Atlantic Ocean. The American people's general respect for animal rights and life is praiseworthy.

Around the globe there are many touching stories and wonderful deeds that prove that the world is not as bad as it seems. What we need from the media is positive reporting and uplifting news, the reporting of events that will change our lives for the better and encourage good social behavior. Let our society be touched with stories of loving kindness and compassion; let our lives be enriched by each other's courage and charity.

Religious integration is a kind of wonderful deed.

Provide Others with Good Causes and Conditions

In this world, there are many worthwhile goals, such as being a law-abiding person in giving, benefiting, and serving others. However, among all these good deeds, none is more important than giving others good causes and conditions.

Giving good causes and conditions is simply helping others in any possible way. If you water the plants in your garden, they flourish beautifully. If you offer grain to birds, they sing wonderfully. If you give encouragement to students or praise teachers, then you provide them with good causes and conditions. You may help promote a good product, or you may help others make achievements in their careers. Sometimes an encouraging look can boost the morale of others. Taking joy in the accomplishments of others and not obstructing them in their endeavors are all simple means of giving good causes and conditions.

There are many actions one can do to give others good causes and conditions. Parents and children, or coworkers and friends, can give each other good causes and conditions. Before Buddha entered into parinirvana, he said, " The sentient beings that have connections with me, I have liberated, and for those who have no connections with me, I have already planted the causes and conditions for them to be delivered."

According to Buddhist history, Chan Master Huineng was able to embark on his path of cultivation to eventually become the patriarch of Chan, because of ten taels of gold from An Daocheng. In the case of Chan Master Linji, he went to learn from Chan Master Gaoan after being prompted by Chan Master Huang Pao to do so. He gained enlightenment, resulting in the proliferation of numerous disciples of the Linji Chan School all over the world.

Because of the induction of his brother, Asanga, Vasubandhu converted to the practice of Mahayana Buddhism and became the shastra master of a thousand treatises.

With only a few words some may provide others with causes and conditions to enter into the Way, or through a written recommendation they may help others to earn a place in history. On his visit to Venerable Master Dadian, the renowned scholar Han Yu of the Tang Dynasty entered into the gate of Dharma upon hearing the Master's attendant say, "First convert by concentration, then liberate by wisdom."

Throughout history, many great leaders have realized their potential because of the good causes and conditions others gave them. Entrepreneurs have garnered the support and help of the skillful and talented people instrumental to their own success because they provided them with causes and conditions and the opportunity to actualize their potential. When it is not harmful to oneself and it is beneficial to others, we should provide others with more opportunities and thus good causes and conditions. It is through building ties and relationships in this way that we are paving the way to our own success, for in giving others benefits we are also benefiting ourselves. So, why don't we become more generous?

The tower provides its light for our safety at night.

The Value of Giving

In this world, the wealthy are those who give freely to others. The poor are those who covet only for themselves. Generally speaking, it is easier to provide for oneself than it is for others; however, if we do not till the land and sow the seeds, we will never reap the harvest. If we do not practice the virtue of "giving," how can we obtain true wealth?

There are, however, two manners of "giving." "Positive" giving is the most wonderful way to give, for it can ensure harmonious interpersonal relationships. A lovely smile, an encouraging word, genuine praise, a little service, or simply giving our warm regards to others can not only beautify our lives, but also purify society. From the moment of birth to the moment of death, we are always on the receiving end of someone else's generosity. Our parents give us unconditional love and care; our teachers give us a chance to gain knowledge and achievements. All kinds of people in society provide us with conditions that are conducive to our daily survival. Now, we must take the time and ask ourselves, what have we done for others in return? What have we given to our families, friends, society and the world?

"Negative" giving, on the other hand, is a common occurrence in society. There are people who give others worries, heartache, embarrassment, and create obstacles without realizing the universal truths in "what goes around comes around" and "do unto others as you would have them do unto you."

Even if we engage in positive giving, there are different levels of positive giving that we can offer. To give money or material possessions is the easiest to accomplish; to give praise or offer caring words is a virtue of higher attainment. But to give the teachings of the Buddha is the greatest gift of all. The giver will acquire unsurpassed merit, while the receiver will have truth, confidence, courage, peace, and ultimate freedom.

"To give unconditionally is the highest virtue, and the most difficult to achieve." Since it is the only form of true giving, we must strive for it wholeheartedly by cultivating the habit of giving without any expectation or return. We must learn to give from our hearts. In our lives, others have created many favorable conditions for us, and we must return their kindness with the same zealousness. For the only way to bring the value of giving into full effect is to establish good conditions and affinities among the world's people and societies. By giving to others, we not only express our gratitude and appreciation, we also plant the seed of fruition.

The ocean is vast, and so gives freely to others.

A Good Sense of Humor

While our material lives in the 21st century have benefited greatly from advancements in science and technology, our spiritual minds have withered away. While our desire for good food has been satisfied, our inherent wisdom has been kept under lock and key.

In today's society, a good sense of humor is the foundation of a happy life, the lubricant of a successful relationship. Only through humor can one be charming and witty; only through humor can one have wisdom and the ability to enjoy what is amusing or comical.

However, we must bear in mind that humor is not sarcasm, but a language of wisdom. Humor is infinite in its profundity and inspiration. Humor is not derision, but a vehicle of self-mockery. A humorous gesture conveys an immeasurable amount of genuine affection and concern.

The intent of humor is not to create embarrassment for others by being overly forward, but to bring happiness to others by lightening or dissolving embarrassing moments. Hence, to have a good sense of humor is to have an enlightened mind, a mind complete with ingenuity, vivacity and intelligence. It is indeed a mental state of unsurpassed carefreeness, without attachments or worries. It is an attitude of complete optimism, when all things past and present can be humorously perceived.

Humor is like a mountain spring, for it can cleanse our mind. It is like a cloud in the sky, for it can wander at will without obstruction. In today's society, people have lost their uniqueness and the ability to think for themselves. Instead of leading, people choose to become followers. Instead of exercising intellectual freedom, they choose to follow the decisions of others. It is society in general and not the individual that decides the common standard of morality. Under these circumstances, it is imperative to have a good sense of humor in our interpersonal relationships, because humor is like sunshine that can brighten our day and bring a smile to our faces. Humor is sometimes like a gentle breeze that can soothe a person's pain and misery. Humor is also like a spring blossom that can warm a person's heart and awaken his or her mind. We should strive to be like Charlie Chaplin, who has brought laughter to millions of moviegoers around the world with his genius for comedy; he has positively affected the lives of many people through his sense of humor.

There have been many eminent Buddhist monks who have possessed an excellent sense of humor. Contemporary Chinese literature is no exception; many authors have the uncanny ability to portray their subjects in a humorous light, without debasing their integrity. Their sense of humor is charming and graceful, which gives readers a refreshing feeling of purity. As we struggle for true peace and happiness in our modern society, we find ourselves in desperate need of a few masters of comedy; those who can enrich the present world with their good sense of humor.

A good sense of humor is the foundation of a happy life.

Take Delight in Shared Joy

Sharing joy with others is not only a virtue, it is also a delightful experience. To take delight in shared joy is to give willing support to those who are compassionate in helping the needy; it is to give genuine praise to those who have dedicated themselves to the highest achievements in life. If we want to be successful in this world, we must cultivate the important virtue of feeling happy when others have done what we cannot do ourselves. The Buddha once said, "If there were really no differentiation between the self and the other, there would be no discrimination between merit acquired from good deeds."

Unfortunately, in today's society there are too many people who take pleasure in the misfortune of others. Instead of practicing the virtue of shared joy, they choose to criticize at will and impart unwarranted abuse. Instead of praising the charity of others, they remark sarcastically that it is just a drop of water in the vast ocean or it is just a boastful act. It is indeed very sad to see that society in general has become so deprived of amiable feelings. It is not surprising that there are very few virtuous people and even fewer virtuous acts.

Something has definitely gone wrong in our society when the majority of our fellow human beings are lacking a good and agreeable nature. Instead of hoping for a better future, it seems like everyone is content waiting for doomsday to approach, when everything in this world will be reduced to nothingness. Why do people indulge themselves in jealous sarcasm and baseless slander? Do we really want to see the end of civilization or the end of our race?

What we need to do is to cultivate and practice the virtue

of shared joy, to give encouragement and exaltation as often as possible. Instead of feeling jealousy or envy, we should instead feel happy for others when they have good fortune. Instead of pity, we should be compassionate and helpful toward those who are less fortunate. Instead of criticizing, we should praise other's good deeds no matter how trivial they might be.

If we really wish to better our country and society, it is imperative for us to foster the virtue of shared joy. We should be willing to cast our vote for political candidates who are dedicated to serving people. We should be happy to give our contributions to those who are devoted to helping the needy. Where there is a need for volunteers, we should put forth all our efforts toward the common goal; where there are good deeds, we should selflessly promote them to achieve a more far-reaching effect.

Since the world of shared joy is a delightful place to be, we should strive to develop the habit of imparting praise, doing good deeds, and supporting worthy causes. If everyone in society can be amiable and pleasant, it will create an atmosphere of great peace, harmony and happiness for all the world's people.

The spring blossom can warm a person's heart.

The Beauty in Magnanimity

Throughout history, there have been great men and women who have forgiven their enemies because they have understood and appreciated the beauty in magnanimity. It is out of generosity and kindness that they have chosen forgiveness over resentment. Therefore, we cannot criticize them as being ignorant of the differences between right and wrong or good and evil. Instead, we should strive to be more like them by releasing our hatred and replacing it with compassion.

During World War II, Japanese soldiers mercilessly murdered the people of Nanjing during the now infamous Nanjing Massacre. Although fifty years have passed, many Chinese people still harbor some form of hostility towards the Japanese people because of their unwillingness to offer a formal apology. The World War II exhibits at the Museum of Tolerance in Los Angeles, California, offer a cruel reminder of how one man's hatred can lead to the loss of six million lives. It is an undeniable fact that hatred has been the main source of unresolved conflicts and war throughout the world, past and present. If an ounce of forgiveness can be found anytime or anywhere, it would be possible for peace to replace animosity in the course of human history. For magnanimity can melt the coldness of hatred like the spring sun can melt the winter snow.

However, few people in the world today are willing to practice the art of forgiveness in appreciation of the beauty of magnanimity. Instead, they choose to take their anger out on innocent victims or severely punish those who have wronged them. If a parent cannot forgive a child's wrongdoing, how can there be love in the family? If a teacher cannot react properly to a student's mistake, how can there be respect in the classroom? If a judge cannot decide a case justly and swiftly, how can there be faith in the legal system? If a policeman cannot be fair and honest, how can there be trust in the police force?

How then can we dissolve hatred and animosity? It is only through loving kindness and compassion that we can find room in our hearts to forgive others. It is only through our willingness to let go of resentment that we can find a way to magnanimity. Words alone will not bring about change. It is only with hearts that are both tolerant and forbearing that we can inspire others to follow our lead and realize the beauty in forgiveness.

In order for a person to rectify his mistakes and to turn his life around, he must be given a second chance. Without the pardon of the law and the people, all is useless. Only when we are willing to accept his apology and forgive his wrongdoing, can we truthfully steer him in the right direction and give him a new lease on life. Therefore, in being magnanimous, we not only bring benefits to others, we also benefit ourselves.

"Those who cannot forbear in small matters will spoil great undertakings" is an old saying that we should take to heart. In order for society to have peace and harmony,

The earth does not deny anything.

each and every one of us must practice the virtue of forbearance and learn to appreciate the beauty in magnanimity. We must not harbor grudges toward others; we must not turn every situation into a federal case. If we can have a heart of forgiveness for our families and friends, our employers and employees, and our governments and society, the world will be a wonderful place to live in, a place of goodness and kindness.

Although the decision "to forgive and forget" can occur in just a thought, it has enormous power in transforming the negative into the positive. By being magnanimous, we can turn violence into peace, hostility into friendship, and disagreement into accord. However, we must put forth all our efforts into cultivating the virtue of magnanimity and inspiring others to do the same. Otherwise, the ideal world of genuine affection and affinity will never be realized.

The Way to Happiness

Everyone in the world is in pursuit of some form of happiness. Some people believe money brings happiness, but money can also bring about abundant suffering and pain. As the Chinese saying goes, "People die for money," just as robbers will often kill for money. During China's Cultural Revolution, most of those who were persecuted were wealthy people. Sometimes the suffering the wealthy endure is far worse than that of the poor.

Then, there are people who believe that love is the source of happiness. Love is beautiful, but love can bring even more suffering. Many tragedies in this world have resulted from people being unable to conquer the hurdle of love. Many have been troubled by love and ruined their careers and reputations as a result. Worse yet, some have killed themselves because of love.

Others believe that fame can enhance happiness, for they believe that those who are famous have the ability to achieve their ambitions. However, many people in high positions often fail to benefit the populace and are only concerned with their own status. In the process, they lose the support of the public and sometimes even of themselves. There are also some people who think they can find happiness in academic studies. But, for most, the deeper their studies, the worse their attachments and discriminations become, giving rise to problems in thought. Instead of resulting in happiness, then, studies can become a dead end.

So, where can we find this happiness we all pursue? First, we must realize that happiness is in our hearts. The contentment, tolerance, wisdom and faith in our hearts are the fountain of happiness inside us. Second, happiness lies in genuine affection and honor. Treating others with sincerity and integrity brings happiness. Third, happiness exists in friendships between the self and others. Nobody can live without friends for friendship provides support and good will throughout our lives. Fourth, happiness is in liberation. For, if we can see through the phenomena of the world, and be liberated from troubles and suffering, then happiness can be realized.

Money does not equal unhappiness; as long as we know how to make good use of it and do not let ourselves become enslaved by it, then money can bring happiness. Similarly, love can also bring happiness; but love needs to be pure and sublime and not selfish or tainted. Social status can also be a source of happiness, if its accomplishments are shared, thus benefiting both the self and others.

We should not only pursue the sensual pleasures of life: seeing beautiful things, hearing wonderful sounds, smelling fragrant scents, tasting delicious food, and feeling physical comforts. Such sensory happiness is only momentary and unrealistic. We should instead be in pursuit of the "joy of non-attachment," meaning that we will not allow ourselves to become attached to the five senses. We should "cultivate our bodhi mind without attachment" to achieve true happiness. It is only when we have the truth and Dharma joy in our hearts, and discover the treasure that lies inside us, that we are able to attain lasting happiness.

The contentment, tolerance, wisdom and faith in our hearts are the fountain of happiness.

Creating Positive and Uplifting Knowledge

When we want to acquire new information, we turn to newspapers or magazines. When we want to hear the most current news, we naturally turn on our television sets - only to be bombarded with rumors and reports of heinous crimes or acts of self-destruction. As Lao Tzu's famous saying goes, is it not better to be uninformed than knowledgeable?

When we start a new job, we are often troubled by scandals and slander, which makes us wonder if it is not better to be ill-informed. When the phone rings, our ears are painfully filled with neighborhood gossip and family feuds, which drive us to seek relief in ignorance.

When husbands get home from a long day's work, instead of peace and quiet, they often have to listen to their wives gripe about the rising cost of groceries or household problems. Often they are confronted with difficult questions from their children regarding the contradictions of the adult world, such as, "Why are government officials always verbally abusing one another when teachers at school teach us to respect one another and to be kind?" What else can one do but sigh deeply and think that ignorance must be bliss.

When we are young, we are motivated by our thirst for knowledge. We study day and night just to achieve good grades. We are like sponges, absorbing knowledge at an incredible rate. When we enter society, however, our thirst has been quenched. This is not because we have obtained all the knowledge there is; instead, it is because we are discouraged by our own experiences. Traps are laid for us everywhere; people are often out to take advantage of us. It seems like the more we learn, the more worried we become.

To have knowledge is supposed to be a wonderful thing. From the present, we can realize the future; from history books, we can know about the past; from scientific research, we can understand the universe; from here, we can become familiar with the unknown. However, we are now faced with the unfortunate situation that "to know" is a frightening experience, without any promise of a better tomorrow.

Although knowledge can bring misery to our lives, we cannot forsake it for a little quiet and peace of mind. Knowledge is still much better than ignorance. What we need to do is to change our perspectives and create positive knowledge. Let our television programs be our vehicles to beautiful scenery and touching stories. Let our newspapers report wondrous deeds and moral acts. Let our governments avoid corruption and administer laws that are beneficial to the people. Let our society be just and kind. Allow us a chance to enjoy the gentle touch of a light breeze and the warmth of the spring sun.

Fo Guang Shan International Translation Center publishes and distributes free Buddhist booklets to the public.

The Importance of Being a Law-Abiding Citizen

Constitution and law are two of the most important factors in maintaining social order and national stability. Without them, disorder and chaos would arise because there would be no agreed-upon contract between us as humans or as citizens. Whenever a group of people is bound together by common interests or beliefs, some form of rules and regulations is necessary to set forth the rights and duties of each individual member.

In the military, there are military laws for every level of personnel and for the organization as a whole. In religious institutions, there are precepts and commandments for the clergy and followers. In a family, there are house rules for children as well as for parents. If a member of any particular group decides to break the established rules of conduct, the cohesiveness of the whole will be threatened.

In a country like the United States, there exists a legislative branch where bills are passed into laws and a judicial branch where the laws are upheld. If a member of Congress or an officer of the Court fails to abide by the established law, the integrity of his or her office will be jeopardized, and he or she will face a vote of no confidence from the general public, or perhaps even removal from office.

In order for a country to run smoothly, there are rules and regulations for every industry. In order for society to survive without chaos, there are laws for almost every aspect of our lives. For example, without election laws, elections would not be fair and just; without banking laws, the economy would be in disarray; without criminal laws, crime would run rampant; and without traffic laws, the streets would become a jungle.

However, at the same time, many people perceive laws as

obstacles to individual liberty and as a means for government to control people. What, then, is the true nature of law? On the surface, rules of conduct, such as precepts or commandments, can be restricting, for they seem to limit the scope of our actions. But in reality, they are the guarantors of personal freedom. For example, if we were to violate any one of the five precepts of Buddhism - no killing, no stealing, no sexual misconduct, no slandering, and no intoxication - we could end up wearing a prison uniform for an extended period of time, depending upon our offense.

Therefore, if a nation desires to achieve long-term stability and prosperity, every one of her citizens must develop the habit of adhering to the laws, as established by custom, agreement, and authority. No one should be allowed to use legal loopholes to avoid problems - not the president, not celebrities, and not ordinary citizens. Everyone should be equal before the law, regardless of race, age, sex, wealth, fame, or position; otherwise, society and the country will fall into utter chaos.

In a country of law and order, in an organization of rules and regulations, nothing is more important than respect for and adherence to the rules. A traffic light is of no value if everyone chooses to ignore its intended meaning. A crosswalk is of no use if everyone chooses to overlook its existence. Only when we stop for a red light or for a pedestrian can traffic lights and crosswalks serve as a means for public safety and a symbol of law. As law-abiding citizens, we must abide by the law and any of its representations, without lapse. As law-abiding citizens, we must act in accordance with the law, without reminder. For without rules and regulations, our country will not prosper, society will be lawless, and our character will be flawed and weakened.

Where is Justice?

Where is justice in nature when only the fittest survive? Where is justice in society when the wealthiest and the most powerful have all the advantages? In this world, it seems natural for the strongest to exert undue power over the weakest. It is no surprise that the rich will oppress the poor, the smart will ridicule the dumb, the old will bully the young, and the healthy will insult the handicapped. Where do we find justice in all of this?

Nowadays, it seems like our lives are full of confusion and contradictions. We no longer have a sharp contrast between black and white, right and wrong. Instead we have gray areas where there is no definite or absolute definition of rightness or fairness. So many judgments are passed on the basis of appearance or family background. If a person comes from a good family, his or her stock immediately rises; if a person comes from the ghetto, his or her stock immediately falls. Since we see the world through an hourglass, where do we expect to find justice?

The situation is even worse in politics, where every decision is based on personal interests or needs. It is common practice for politicians to forego public welfare in the interest of big corporations. We do not need to look any further than a candidate's campaign finances, of which most of the money is made up of funds from big companies and special interest groups. Therefore, a promise to the voters is just an empty promise, a ploy to gain election or re-election. When a promise goes unfulfilled, how many times have we seen elected officials making excuses, or placing the blame on others? Do we honestly think that there is justice in politics or government?

Where is justice when money and power and fame and

fortune are deciding factors in society? Where is justice when the wealthy can push their way through everything, while the poor must suffer indignity? Where is justice when cheating is allowed and honesty is punished? Where is justice when selfishness is praised and lending a helping hand is ridiculed? Where is justice when the weak are bullied and the aggressors are feared? Where is justice in this world of inequality?

Someone once said, "Unreasonableness cannot win over reason, rationality cannot take precedence over law, legality cannot defeat power, and nothing is more superior than universal truth." What is the "universal truth" that reigns over everything else? It is the law of karma, based on the principle of causation. No matter who or what you are in life, no one can escape karma or death, for the law of cause and effect applies equally to every living being. According to the Buddha's teachings, karma or volitional activity bears fruit in accordance with whether one's actions have been wholesome or not. It is a natural process, unsupervised and undisturbed by any supernatural power or force. By increasing our credit balance of good deeds, we alone have the ability to modify the course of karma.

Therefore, it is imperative for everyone to understand how karma works, for true justice resides in karma. Neither money nor power can alter the course of karma; neither fame nor fortune can change the result of karma. A doer of bad deeds will always reap the fruit of retribution, while a doer of wholesome deeds will always reap the fruit of goodness. In the end, no one is exempt from the universal truth of karma and causation.

Illicit Possessions

In this world of ours, there are so many incidents in which people, especially those in authority or high positions, abuse the privileges of their offices for their own profit. The pursuit of wealth and prosperity is something everyone desires, but those who are avaricious are insatiable in their endless craving for more, and will stop at nothing to obtain their possessions illicitly. These people would steal, take bribes, default on their debts, embezzle, cheat, and take advantage of any opportunity to make a profit. In order to earn a fortune, some might even engage in illicit businesses, such as gambling and prostitution, or in other kinds of scams.

Should someone make money by any of the above means, they certainly could not escape retribution in accordance with the laws of cause and effect. Fortune gained from such means rarely lasts very long. Throughout history, many people who were crafty enough to cheat and steal, to abuse their power and take graft appeared to have been successful in their racketeering, but ended up losing all they had, including their precious lives, ultimately earning nothing but infamy. So what is there to be gained from such illicit activities?

In our daily lives, we often unknowingly take things that were not given to us, such as casually picking a flower from a bush in the park. It may appear trivial, but it is important to realize that all sorts of theft and robbery start from the habit of taking small things! There is a story in which a teacher tells a parent, "Your son stole his classmate's pencil." Furiously, the father slapped his child and scolded, "How could you steal from others? If you needed pencils, I could have just grabbed a bunch from my office for you!" Though this is only a joke, such incidents do often take place around us. It is the small things in life that we should be vigilant about. So we should all be mindful that we can own as much as we want lawfully but should never possess anything illicitly!

A Gilded Dinner Table

In the dining hall of a Buddhist temple there are a few round tables that seat ten people each. They are made of wood, nicely painted and trimmed with a golden-colored aluminum strip. Upon seeing the tables, one devotee criticized, "Temples should practice simplicity. How can they use such luxurious dinner tables to treat their guests?" Those who heard his words considered the criticism to be true, but actually this devotee's views are extremely ignorant and crude!

Though Buddhism does not consider materialism as important, it still recognizes the need for material goods in this world for adornment. In a temple, if the Buddha Hall were not magnificent and auspicious, who would come to worship? If statues of the Buddha were not gilded with gold, who would come to pay homage? In the Western Pure Land of Ultimate Bliss, its verandas and gazebos are adorned with the seven jewels for those who wish to be reborn there. If only crude furnishings were used to receive dinner guests, would you like to come?

Simple living is a demand we make of ourselves, but should not impose on others. So if after enjoying a delicious meal in a beautiful setting, we still criticize the temple for its standards, are we displaying our Buddha Nature? When most people only understand half of what they see and fail to comprehend what the other half is about, their views are often shallow and crude.

Another case in point: after a meal is served, if the attendants remove and dispose of the leftovers, the devotee above might have criticized the temple for being wasteful since the leftovers could have been used for the next meal. Even if disposing of the leftovers sounds reasonable, those who hear the criticism might agree with the speaker. But if, for the sake of cherishing what you have, you were invited to use the leftovers from the previous guests, would you share the same view? If anyone were to get sick from eating leftovers in a temple, the media would blow the incident out of proportion and accuse the temple of spreading disease. Would you consider it fair and reasonable then?

The magnificent and auspicious Buddha Hall attracts many people to Fo Guang Shan in Kaoshiung, Taiwan.

    Therefore, before we make demands of others, we should first make demands of ourselves; if we fall short we should not impose our standards on others. Instead, we should reproach ourselves the way we would others and forgive others the way we would ourselves. Otherwise the fault of such speech karma would offset any merit previously cultivated. In this regard, can we afford not to be cautious?

How To Change Fate

What we often care most for in life is the "self," and the most important aspect of self is none other than fate. In one's lifetime, fate is changed frequently because of circumstances that arise. Because of a person, an event, a word, a dollar, or even a thought, some may change their entire life. Similarly, the development of a country may be changed and the history of humankind may even be re-written.

Britain's Duke of Windsor abdicated his throne in order to be with his beloved, Mrs. Wallis Simpson. In giving up his kingdom for his wife, he changed his life because of a woman and also re-wrote the history of his country. Former U.S. President Richard Nixon lost the most important job in the world over the Watergate scandal. So while our position may bring us high esteem, an event may lead us to shameful humiliation.

Chan Master Danxia of the Tang Dynasty intended to travel to the Chinese capital for the national examinations, but he met a monastic on his way who told him, "It is better to be tested for Buddhahood than for a position as an imperial official." He was awakened from his dream of fame and fortune and opened up a whole new life for himself instead. Henry Ford's father gave him a dollar when he left home to strike out on his own. He used that dollar as capital and eventually built the Ford Company, making a name for himself in history and benefiting all of humankind in the process.

Tang Dynasty's Venerable Master Xuanzang studied the Buddhist scriptures when he was young and felt that the translations of sutras was insufficient at the time. He took the initiative to go to India to bring back more sutras. Because of this single thought, he spent eighteen years in India and brought back thousands of volumes of scriptures. He became known as the Master of the Buddhist Canon. His intention changed his life, and turned a new page in the development of Chinese Buddhism, History and Culture.

Each person's life is different from the next person's. When we see others flying high while we are down, we inevitably sigh, and complain that it is just not the best time in our lives, or even blame the heavens for our ill fate. But others may take life as it is, thinking that all of life's fortunes are pre-destined.

In reality, our fate is not controlled by anyone. Fate is the result of karma, and anything from habit, religion, emotions, power, or desire can affect fate. Therefore, regardless of whether it concerns people, money or affairs, we need only to cultivate the right view, establish faith in religion, build good connections with people, and strictly observe the precepts; then we will not be controlled by fate but can instead freely improve our fate.

Venerable Master Xuanzang took the initiative to go to India to bring back more Buddhist sutras.

All in a Thought

When we talk about time, we often say "time flies;" however, our thoughts are like lightning, moving even faster than time. Our minds are like the ocean, thoughts rolling in and crashing like waves, one after another, never ceasing.

Our minds are not limited by time and space. We can travel the world in a thought; we can experience three lifetimes in a thought. We can go up to heaven and then back down to earth, all in a thought. Our minds can be as large as the universe, encompassing realms as numerous as grains of sand in the desert. As the Chinese saying goes, "When we have no worries on our minds, a small bed is as large as the universe. But when we have trouble on our minds, the world can become very small." Our minds can embrace three thousand realms in just a single thought. Be it heaven or hell, rebirth in the six realms, or a Buddha or a demon, it can all be in a thought.

Our mind is our master, for from our minds arise views. If we change our views and our outlook in life, we can change our fate. A thought can change tears into smiles; a thought can transform foolishness into wisdom. A thought of compassion to help others elicits the mind of sages, but a thought of jealousy to hurt others brings forth the mind of the wicked. A thought of selfishness to profit oneself can only result in limited accomplishments, but a thought of initiative to benefit others can attain limitless merit.

Throughout history, a simple thought has changed the fate of many countries. Kings and emperors have risen and fallen as a result of a single thought, and their countries have followed suit. In this world, many people change their entire lives on the basis of a hasty decision. Many take their own lives for lost love, leaving their families in pain and grief, while some steal and kill for profit, bringing others great harm, and ruining their own lives as well. All of these things can happen in a single thought.

Our minds hold the key to our rise and fall. There are two sides to every thought; we can be liberated and let go of all worries on a thought of enlightenment, or we can be entrapped, and create waves of agitation on a thought of delusion. The mind is also a symbol of eternity. A thought of enlightenment can transform. A thought of delusion affects our entire life, and in a moment of passion, it can become the guide to our next life. A thought, then, can be so crucial. As practitioners, should we not be cautious of all that is in a thought?

A Buddha or a demon can all be in a thought.

Overcoming Fear

We all have fears. We fear the future when we suffer losses of property and money; if we feel the pain of physical injury or if our lives are threatened, the fear may be even stronger. When our lives are in danger, we may be willing to give anything to save our precious lives, depending on the strength of our fear. Some people are afraid of wild animals, such as lions and tigers, while others fear demons and spirits; some are afraid of being alone, while others may fear darkness. To put it simply, at one time or another in life we all feel fear .

Children fear being punished by their parents; women fear being abandoned by their men for another woman; merchants fear failure in business; and politicians fear public opinion and its consequences. Students are afraid of tests, and soldiers may fear wars; some are afraid of traffic accidents, while others fear robbers. There are those who fear the justice of heaven and the way of human relations. Of all these fears, cause and effect and retribution from karma should be feared more than anything else.

Everyone fears natural and man-made disasters: typhoons, war, fire, floods, earthquakes, or even the flash of lightning and the roar of thunder. We are also afraid of adversities in human relationships, such as slander, rumor, gossip, and sabotage. Some may consider the heavens fearsome, but actually worldly affairs are worse. Others may think ghosts are scary, but actually people are even scarier. Some worry about the hardships of life, while others agonize over the decline in health caused by aging and illness. Children have their own fears, just as seniors have their own troubles. Those in power may seem fearless in public, but may be hen-pecked at home; great heroes are usually full of courage and good spirit, but they still have to face the suffering caused by illness.

Fearing heavenly justice and the principle of cause and effect is not always bad, for that would prevent people from wrongdoing and committing bad deeds. If we are in a constant state of fear about other things, then we may not treat others well. Instead, we should develop a strong, honest character. The *Heart Sutra* teaches us that, in order to be free from fear, we need to enhance our wisdom. We should understand and see through illusions, and bravely take on the obstacles we face. The *Universal Gate Chapter of the Lotus Sutra* also teaches us that those who are weak and fearful should recite the name of the "Avalokitesvara" Bodhisattva, because Avalokitesvara is also named the "Giver of Fearlessness." As long as we recite the name of the Bodhisattva and accept the Bodhisattva's gift of "fearlessness," why should there be any more fear in life?

A bird flies in the sky, and it does not fear any difficulty.

Ridding Ourselves of Stress

In this modern world, people are constantly saying, "Life is too stressful!" Why are people so stressed out? How can we rid ourselves of stress? Students feel stressed because of heavy schoolwork; parents feel stressed because they have too many chores and family obligations; policemen feel stressed because they have too much work; workers feel stressed and are unhappy because their work hours are too long.

Stress - it is the same for everyone, regardless of age. We all feel the impact of stress in our daily lives. Tenants cannot afford to pay rent at the end of the month. Parents think their children do not listen to them and feel pressured by the task of raising them. Husbands and wives are suspicious of one another, skeptical of their relationships as well as the faithfulness of their partners. They experience stress in marriage. Grocers are challenged by business competition, and street-sweepers are repulsed by the filthiness every morning they go to work.

Actually many things around us contribute to stress in our daily lives; for instance, stress from disappointments, obstacles, poverty, our jobs, ailments, relationships, and even death. Stress is everywhere. There are even sources of stress inside us; for example, stress from feeling emptiness, jealousy, depression, hatred, ignorance, evil thoughts, and vengeance. Taken together, the stresses of everyday life seem insurmountable.

However, stress does not only result from negative matters. Good things in life can also be stressful, such as stress from possessions, beauty, power, gratitude, success, and so forth. The seemingly endless universe is limited, but stress is truly limitless. Some people are overwhelmed by stress and yield to physical fatigue, poor motivation, suicidal tendencies, or mental confusion. If you would like to rid yourself of stress, the following are some recommendations:

1. *Enhance your knowledge and wisdom by observing and learning from what happens around you. By gaining further knowledge and deepening your understanding, you can reduce stress.*
2. *Be optimistic, cheerful and carefree! Open your heart as wide as the ocean, so you can embrace the universe. Be optimistic about everything and do not overburden yourself, and you will eventually alleviate stress.*
3. *Develop the ability to let go. Like a piece of luggage, carry it only when you need it. However, when you do not need it, put it away and let go. Do not compare or calculate, and you will eventually dissipate stress.*
4. *Befriend stress. Be willing to accept stress as a part of you and a part of life. Why bother fighting it?*
5. *Make use of every opportunity to rest and go with the flow. When you do not ask for stress or resent it, stress will eventually disappear.*
6. *Place more emphasis enhancing patience, compassion and wisdom by cultivating the self. Let us train ourselves to challenge and take on stress. Then it will eventually be dispelled.*

Every Buddhist should cultivate concentration, wisdom, right thoughts and good reasoning. There is a Chinese saying, "When enemy troops invade, the commanding generals resist; when floods come, the earth will counter." So, where is stress?

Beauty and Ugliness

Everyone loves beauty and detests ugliness. In this world, there are people who have a beautiful appearance but have the heart of a beast; and there are people who are unattractive but have a very compassionate heart. There are luxurious and elegant mansions inhabited by greedy and corrupt politicians, but there exist dilapidated homes inhabited by those with honesty and integrity. There are many things in the world that are beautiful on the surface but ugly within, and, conversely, there are things that are ugly on the outside but beautiful on the inside. Some things are neither beautiful nor ugly. It should not matter if we find something unattractive, but we should be wary of the ugliness that can lie within. Naturally, we always want the world to be beautiful; however, it is more important to possess a beautiful mind.

When we speak of beauty, we can speak of two kinds of beauty: natural beauty and artificial beauty. The beauty of nature is superior to any artificial beauty, for the latter is just the creation of humans. There are some who can write beautifully, while others can speak beautifully, and still others can paint beautifully. Some people can create a beautiful environment, while others can fashion a beautiful physique and aura. So, wise friends, do you adore beauty? How much effort have you put into beautifying your surroundings? How often do you ask yourself, do I speak and comport myself beautifully? Do I act and behave beautifully? Do I receive and greet others beautifully? Do I think and conduct myself beautifully?

True beauty comes from within. Only a good heart will bring about beautiful things; only a true heart will turn out beautiful things; only a compassionate heart will beget beautiful things;

and only a pure heart will lead to beautiful things. It is therefore our common wish to create a beautiful world and a beautiful life, and similarly, we all want to establish a beautiful environment and a beautiful home.

Many Japanese have felt shame about their recent past and the notoriety of being the "ugly" Japanese. But don't the Chinese often feel the same way? And, at one time or another, haven't other people of the world had similar feelings? It is better for us to realize and understand our capacity for ugliness, for the problem lies in not knowing. Without self-awareness, we will never be able to improve. But if we know that we are ugly, we can change ourselves and behave beautifully. When we know we are ugly, we can feel ashamed of ourselves, but then we can work to become beautiful naturally. We should realize that a beautiful appearance is difficult to maintain over time, but a beautiful heart will last forever. The first step, then, toward being beautiful is to speak good words, do good deeds and to have good thoughts. By following these three rules, let us all start to beautify our world !

The pure and beautiful lotus grows out of the filthy mud.

The Unsurpassed Value of Impermanence

Birth and death are realities of life. Regardless of who we are, we cannot escape either one. While birth is celebrated, death is feared by most. In order to cope with our fear, we often seek comfort in religion.

Although each of the world's major religious traditions has its own teaching concerning death, Buddhism is the only one that promotes the doctrine of impermanence as one of the universal truths. However, it is a truth that is not embraced by all. The majority of people chose to ignore or refute it, due to a lack of understanding or insight. As a result, "impermanence" has become a forbidden word in everyday living.

According to the Buddha's teaching, impermanence is, in fact, a good phenomenon. Because of impermanence, there can be hope in the future. Because of impermanence, there can be happiness without suffering. Imagine a world without change, where everything stays the same forever. Do we really want to live in that kind of a world? If the answer is no, then we should value the Buddhist doctrine of impermanence. However, we must understand that the outcome of change can be either good or bad, depending on the causes and conditions at hand.

When we have a complete understanding of impermanence, we will learn to treasure the value of our lives, our possessions and our friendships. When we witness a seed turning into a tall tree, we will come to appreciate the significance of change. On the other hand, when we see a flower withering as the seasons change, we will experience the downside of impermanence. Through impermanence, everything is possible. The negative can be transformed into the positive, and the positive turned into the negative. With hard work, the poor can become rich, the unenlightened enlightened. Without change, democracy would never be able to overthrow dictatorship; civilization could never have replaced barbarism. Because of impermanence, we do not have everlasting fame, fortune or good health. Therefore, it is not wise to become too attached to our possessions. We should instead be aware of the truth in impermanence, and in our endeavors seize the moment.

"Impermanence" is a universal Law of Nature in addition to being a doctrine of Buddhism. Classical writers have long expressed their reflections on impermanence in their prose and poetry. "Where the grass and weeds grow idly, the soldiers and war horses once roamed. As the wind blows and the water flows, where did the heroes go?" Although impermanence, suffering and emptiness are facts of life, by preparing the mind for enlightenment and the ultimate realization of the truth, they can be transcended. As long as we are strong in our resolve to reach the final stage of cultivation- nirvana - we will be able to overcome change and find the path to true freedom without attachments.

Why does the leaf stand alone? Where have the rest of the leaves gone?

Between Success and Failure

In this world, many people are afraid of failure. They fear the prospect of not being successful because "success" is viewed by most as the object of admiration and "failure" the object of contempt. Therefore, people put forth all their efforts in pursuit of "success;" but between "success" and "failure," how many are truly satisfied with what they have or have not achieved?

How, then, is "success" measured in ordinary terms? In business, success is profit and lost capital is failure. In science, an experiment is a success if it achieves the expected result; otherwise, it is a failure. In battle, victory equals success and defeat equals failure. In the investigation of a crime, when the case is solved, it is a success; if it remains unsolved, it is a failure.

Therefore, the desirability of a given outcome and a certain level of achievement measure "success" and "failure." If we receive a good grade on a test, we consider it a success. If a candidate wins an election, he or she considers the campaign a worthwhile effort. If a movie bombs at the box office, it is seen as a failure. Although "success" is the object of our pursuits, we do not understand its attainment. Most people do not understand what it takes to be successful in life. They relegate success and failure to external causes and conditions, as if they have no control over what happens to them. They credit success to good fortune and failure to bad luck. They do not seem to understand that the key to success or failure lies within each of us.

In reality, there are no absolute definitions of "success" and "failure." What seems to be a success may turn out to be a failure, and vice versa. When he was young, Sir Isaac Newton's teachers treated him as if he was not too bright, but he later became one of the most influential scientists of all time. At the height of the Roman Empire, Julius Caesar was the most powerful figure in the western world, but his fellow countrymen later assassinated him. In 1972, Richard Nixon won the presidential election by a huge landslide, but shortly thereafter, he was forced to resign the presidency because of the Watergate scandal.

According to the Buddha's teaching, "effect is determined by cause and condition." If we desire a certain result, we must first cultivate the right causes and conditions. If we wish to have a good harvest, we must first till the land and sow the seed. Nothing is free in this world; we must work for everything. In order to be successful, we must create the right causes and conditions, for without them, success will not come about. Therefore, to determine "success" or "failure," it is up to us to decide what kind of effort we are willing to put forth in our endeavors. How, then, can we not be careful of the choices we make in life?

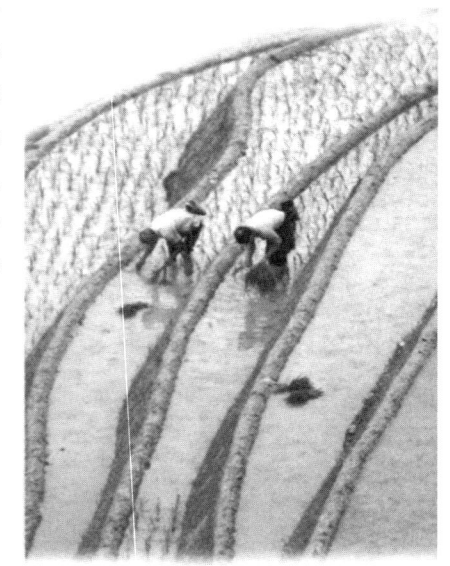

If we wish to have a good harvest, we must first till the land and sow the seed.

A Carefree Life

There are many different ways to lead our lives. Some prefer to dedicate their lives to serving others, while others prefer to lead a self-centered life. Others may lead a life of wisdom, a life of ignorance, a life of happiness, or a life of worries. There are also those who spend their lives alone, indulging in food and drink. Like horses and cows, they have no desire other than to be fed water and hay. Others live in worlds of endless desire, subservient to greed and enslaved by lust. There are only a limited few who truly want to lead a carefree life and be liberated from all defilements.

Look at this world! There are many who cannot live a carefree life because of money, lust, illusion, fame or power. Throughout our lives, we are constantly fanned by the eight winds: praise, ridicule, slander, fame, gain, loss, sorrow, and joy. These winds provoke us daily. There seems to be no escape from the suffering they cause. We allow these winds to become a part of our lives, controlling our minds. Thus, it is extremely difficult to maintain a carefree mind.

In order to attain a carefree mind, we must learn to place ourselves in the shoes of others and to change our perspective. If we can look at things from another person's point of view, then problems can be easily resolved. We can all enjoy peace then. We need to learn to look at things from different angles; we should not automatically expect others to place us ahead of their own interests. We should criticize and tolerate others as we would criticize and tolerate ourselves. When there is equanimity and magnanimity, a carefree life can be realized.

For instance, when others cheat us out of our life savings, we should understand that we probably owed them something in a past life. It is only fair for us to pay off any debts from a previous life in this one. By understanding this, we can become carefree. When our loved ones leave us, no matter how resentful or reluctant we are, we must learn to reflect. If we love them, we should respect their freedom. If they are free, how can we not let ourselves be "carefree" too? When power is lost, we need not agonize, for, without power, our spirit is lifted. When our minds are liberated, how can we not be carefree? When we are slandered, we should not feel humiliated. Just think of it as a means of eradicating our bad karma. Instead of harboring hatred for those who harm us, we should learn to thank them for ridding us of our misfortunes. Under the circumstances, how can we not feel carefree?

Life is just another manufacturer. The type of products you want to manufacture depends on you. If your production line manufactures products such as good reasoning, mindfulness, benevolence and selflessness, then you will earn a good name. How can your life not be carefree then? A carefree life is not dependent upon others. It is not granted by another super-being. To be carefree is our own business. We can turn our knowledge to wisdom, and change ourselves from being self-centered to magnanimous. We can change sorrow to joy, and ignorance to enlightenment. Then our repressed lives can become carefree!

A carefree life is dependent upon self - not others.

The True Meaning of Love

Love has many faces - selfish or unconditional, defiled or pure, finite or infinite, and vulgar or transcendent. Love is an instinct. It can give us strength and hope, but it must comply with morality and law for it to be invaluable.

Everything would be impossible if there were no love. We need love in order to have broad affinities with others and a heart of gold. There must be love between husband and wife, parents and children, and between friends. We must strive to be like a bodhisattva, who has loving kindness and compassion for all beings. There would be no order or morality if there were no love, because love maintains our personal relationships and establishes the differences between friends and families.

Love is not a one-way street. True love is not a possession; it is a sacrifice. If we truly love someone, we must help him or her to accomplish everything in life and wish him or her the best of luck. However, we must have some discretion with love. There must be differentiation among the objects of our love. Truth, justice and goodness should be on the top of our list, whereas lies, injustice and evil should always be excluded. We should also strive to broaden the scope of our love. The objects of our love should not only include our loved ones, our country, our world, and the peace of our race.

Looking at today's society, we see few examples of true love. What we see are distortions and abuses of love. Instead of true love, there is lust and greed. Without good causes and conditions, love can instigate crime; it can bring harm to us, as well as to others. For example, misplaced love between men and women can result in adultery or illicit affairs.

In order to have long-lasting love, we must first cultivate good causes and conditions. We must learn to have the right kind of love, love that can lead to the fulfillment of truth, beauty and goodness. In true love, we must use compassion to purify the objects of our love. In true love, we must use wisdom to lead our loved ones in the right direction. In true love, we must use kindness and goodness to help others accomplish their goals. In true love, we must use morality to protect every living being. Since the meaning of life comes from love, we must use true and purified love to dignify this wonderful world of ours.

The Value of Perception

Perception is a relative concept. It is relative to time and space. For example, our perception of a freeway during the morning rush hour is different than it is in midday traffic. The freeway seems wider and faster midday, but in reality, it is the same freeway as it is in the morning. What has changed is our perception, not the object of our perception. It is human nature to seek the good and avoid the bad, to have pleasant feelings instead of unpleasant ones. Therefore, it is natural for us to look for beauty amidst decay, comfort amidst misery. As the seasons change from winter to spring, our moods will change accordingly from despair to hope. We anxiously search for the feeling of spring by visiting gardens and watching the flowers bloom. It is this perception of spring that guides us in our lives and helps us through the darkest time, allowing us to cast aside feelings of suffering.

In our search for the good and beautiful, we are willing to endure all kinds of unpleasantness, because beauty can replenish our minds and sharpen our senses. We see people sitting impatiently in their cars during rush hour traffic, but waiting patiently to gain entrance into Yosemite National Park. This change of attitude can be readily explained. It is the anticipated wonder of nature's creations that brings a sense of tranquility to the minds of visitors, that enables them to enjoy and appreciate nature's beauty once they set foot inside the park. It is the perception of beauty that can transform a person's mind from agitation to calmness, opening a person's heart to goodness and hope for the future.

Perception does not come from without; it comes from within. It is not a thing that we can buy with money or create on a whim. It is the door to the innermost part of our minds, the bridge to enlightenment through the medium of mental tranquility and right thoughts. As long as we can calm our minds, we will have a garden or spring within ourselves, without having to wait for the seasons to change. As long as we have right thoughts in our minds, we will see the truth and not become victims of delusion. We will cease to create karma that will result in future retribution.

Therefore, it is imperative for us to strengthen our perceptions and mental states, to cultivate the habits of contemplation and introspection. Only when we have realized the ultimate Truth and perceived worldly phenomena as they are will enlightenment be possible in this world of constant flux. At the moment of awakening, we will experience the coming of spring, when flowers will suddenly come into full bloom and trees will unexpectedly unfold their buds. Our lives will turn over a new leaf, our perception will be devoid of illusions, and our minds will be forever purified.

Perception does not come from without; it comes from within.

Have Respect for Life

    Life is the most precious thing in the world, so it is imperative that we respect it in all its forms. Not only must we have regard for human life, we must also respect animal life and the life of any organism in our ecosystem. The worst offense a person can ever commit is to violate the life of others, or even to cause harm to the environment.

    Unfortunately, in today's society, respect has become a foreign concept and consideration a forgotten notion. A moment of selfish intention can lead to the loss of life; a moment of unexplained hatred can result in cruel and unusual punishment. It is no surprise then that today's headlines are full of senseless crimes. It seems as though taking "a life, any life," has become a common occurrence in everyday living. Indifference has replaced sympathy and loving kindness.

    Although human beings like to think of themselves as civilized people, their actions and thoughts are often barbaric. Instead of settling their disagreements over a cup of tea or coffee, they choose to do it with guns and violence. Instead of satisfying their hunger with plain rice and vegetables, they choose to eat a fancy meal full of poultry and seafood. "To repay any debt owed" is a common-sense practice, but how can we ever repay a life, lost due to our selfish desires?

    The Buddha has taught us that there is no differentiation between the "self" and the "other," because every living being is made up of five aggregates - form, feeling, perception, mental formations, and consciousness. There is no permanent, everlasting self, for everything is in a constant state of flux. If we want to inject meaning into our existence, we must first acknowledge the existence of others, because the self in isolation is meaningless. We, as human beings, exist as elements of a vast network of relationships with other beings. Not only do I exist for others, others exist for me. It is for both humans and others that I can be human, that I may enter the realm of meaning. However, there is also a reciprocal dependency of others on me, which constitutes a perpetual two-way interaction between living things. Consequently, if I deny the existence of others, I myself, will be thrown into the abyss of non-existence.

When we come to understand this relationship of mutual dependency between the self and the other, we will be able to perceive the interests of others as our own. We will acquire a sense of inviolability and dignity regarding the existence of others in that when we truly understand our relationship with them, they cease to be expendable and become necessary to our being. Therefore, we must have respect for their right to live.

In actuality, humans are not the only ones who live and breathe. Plants, grass, rivers, and mountains are also full of vitality. When we waste a paper cup so we can have one drink of water, we are throwing away something of value. We are committing an act that is devoid of compassion. We must learn to treasure everything in nature, and all of its byproducts. We must learn to cultivate the virtue of temperance and not be wasteful in front of our children. We must teach them the value of life at an early age for the sake of preventing them from taking a life when they grow up. For it is just a short step away from killing an insect for fun to murdering another human being out of disrespect.

It is truly sad to see that the human race as a whole has come to the point where it has little regard for the value of life. Not only do we violate the rights of others in order to live, some of us also take our own lives. Suicide is not only an act of stupidity, it is also an act of selfishness that will result in karmic retribution of the worst kind. It is indeed very troublesome and frustrating to see people's refusal to treasure life as they should. Why can't we just have a little more respect and consideration for others as well as ourselves?

Life is the most precious thing in the world, so it is imperative that we respect each other.

To Live in Peace and Quiet

During morning rush hour and afternoon traffic jams, we sit anxiously in our cars as the freeways become a giant parking lot. From high-rise buildings, in our small cubicles, we stare blankly at our computer terminals, as the clock ticks away. We often feel trapped and search for a way out of this life. Where do we find a peaceful place to dwell amidst the concrete jungle of today's world? Where do we look for peace and quiet amidst the noise of today's society? As we hustle and bustle aimlessly through life, the gentle touch of a spring breeze and the warmth of the summer sun seem to be eons away.

According to Buddhist texts, we should not seek to dwell on form, sound, smell, taste, touch, or in the things we perceive because all things in existence, material or immaterial, are subject to decay and destruction. As time progresses, our bodies will weaken; as we grow older, our health will deteriorate. The condition of our houses will dissipate with time, and repairs will be as constant as the passing years. Our wealth will increase or decrease depending on the ever-changing economy; and our love will fade, because nothing lasts forever. Since everything is impermanent, where should our bodies and minds take abode?

Throughout the history of Buddhism, many eminent monks have taken drastic steps in search of true peace and quiet. The second patriarch of the Chan School was willing to sacrifice one of his arms for the sake of finding a way to calm his body and mind. The sixth patriarch rediscovered his true Buddha Nature and attained enlightenment when he finally gained insight into the truth behind "finding one's nature by not dwelling in anything." Therefore, true peace and quiet will only come about when we are not deliberately seeking a place to dwell in the material or immaterial. Only when we have achieved peace of mind will our lives be fulfilled and happy. Once a reporter asked President Truman how he could remain so calm under pressure, and the President replied, "It is because I have a safe harbor in my heart."

The problem with people today is that they insist on finding their abode in greed, hatred and ignorance. They feel agitated and unsettled because their lives are full of worry and insecurity. Instead of following the right path to a carefree life, they choose to dwell on gossip and scandals. They enjoy taking advantage of others and ignoring the truth behind the saying, "What goes around comes around." Everyday they spend countless hours looking for ways to satisfy their insatiable desires, without realizing that true happiness lies in simple contentment. Every night, they lie awake, in fear of retribution, not knowing that the only way to a life without worry is to understand the law of causation.

What then is the path to a life of peace and quiet? We should give ourselves to society and work to benefit our fellow human beings. We should find our abode in the Law of Nature, and respect the lives of other living beings. We must not go against nature and the workings of karma. We must dwell in loving kindness, compassion, shared joy, and equanimity. Only in ultimate Truth will harmony and tranquility prevail.

The Buddha taught us, "Our thoughts are like swift currents, and our minds are thus unsettled." Ordinary people abide in the five senses; sages abide in purity and the joy of the Dharma. However, the bodhisattvas make their abode where there are no doubts or defilements, and consider it their duty and responsibility to benefit others.

Therefore, in seeking peace and quiet, we must not only

have a good environment for our physical bodies, we must also have a pure abode for our minds. We must establish a good relationship with our neighbors and urge the improvement of our social customs. We must strengthen our education system and promote understanding of our culture. We must instill family values and advocate morality by way of religious practice. Only when our bodies are at ease and our minds at peace will our lives be truly satisfying and fulfilled.

The Main Shrine of Fo Guang Shan is located in Kaoshiung, Taiwan.

Establish Yourself

A country requires the establishment of a national defense to achieve peace and stability. It needs culture and education to accomplish harmony and civilization. It must have an economic system in place to attain wealth and affluence. And it requires the establishment of transportation systems to have prosperity and development. Individuals also need to establish themselves so that the path of life can be broadened and the meaning of life can flourish.

To establish yourself is to strengthen yourself, to develop your potential, to grow and mature, to establish confidence, to revise your views, to correct your bad habits, to nurture causes and conditions, to create opportunities, and to build up your career and success. In today's society, many people seem to have lost themselves. Many seek or require external help. If a person relies completely on others and has no inner strength, once the help is gone he or she may lose the ability to move on. Therefore, we should establish ourselves as our own engineers in life and live our lives to the fullest.

However, there are people who do not know how to establish themselves, but instead sabotage and destroy themselves by ruining their health, wasting time, failing to build relationships, giving up opportunities, being lazy and slothful, or becoming pessimistic and unrealistic. A few years ago, in the effort to win a gold medal by eliminating the competition, Tonya Harding, an American figure skater, hired someone to assault her competitor. In the end, not only did she fail to win the top prize, she also lost her reputation and found herself in serious legal trouble. Ms. Harding's scheme to strike down another in order to achieve success not only injured another but also ruined her. Thus, to establish ourselves, we should begin by establishing our own minds.

As we see in many elections today, candidates often take every opportunity to attack their competitors, often involving themselves in mudslinging before they publish their own platform for candidacy. Under the circumstances, we cannot help but worry about the future of the country. Hopefully, future candidates will no longer trouble voters with their antics, but will instead let them happily cast their vote for the right candidate.

According to Chinese battle strategy, it is believed that "establishing the mind is more important then establishing a defense." To establish one's mind is to establish right thoughts, right views, ethical values and moral principles. It is important to establish confidence and to be positive about our knowledge, ability, initiatives and compassion. Furthermore, we should also have self-respect, inner strength and initiative.

We should often review our own moral code, our speech and our responsibilities. Striving for perfection in these three things is the ultimate goal in establishing oneself. It is imperative that we should be the first to shoulder life's burdens but be the last to enjoy its benefits, instead of aiming to ruin others in order to achieve purely selfish goals.

Mountains sustain the growth of forests, support the lives of fowl and beasts, and allow creatures to congregate and live freely.

Live Courageously

To crave death is a trait of weakness; to strive to live is courageous. Life should be "alive," and we can only appreciate the colors of life when we are alive. On the other hand, death is like the sunset, for even when there are signs of life, there is no more brightness in the world. Many people suffer business losses and all but run out of hope, but they continue to strive courageously to succeed. As long as they develop their potential in life, they will naturally encounter the right conditions to help them overcome their difficulties. They will be able to stand up on their feet and get on the road to success again. Many others endure lost love. Heartbroken, they lack the courage to carry on. But they need to understand that, just as there are numerous stars in the sky, there are even more people on earth. Why suffer so much for one person? Instead, they should pull themselves together and begin a new life.

Arriving at a seemingly dead-end road may actually signify the beginning of a new one. In our world, many survive the pain and horrors of natural calamities, yet they continue to live. The courage they display in the face of loss and suffering makes them models for others who face life's trials and tribulations.

Because of impermanence, nothing escapes the tide of change. Both the good and the bad come with impermanence and change, so there is always hope as long as we live. Therefore, whether we suffer business failure, lost love, a family dispute, financial difficulty, a career setback, or poor health, we must live on courageously. In face of hopelessness, we should still maintain hope to the very end.

Likewise, in the battlefield, even when the troops are

"down to the last man," they still fight on for their country. In nature's world, cold ashes may burn again, and dead wood may sprout to life. The chance to survive often hangs on the brink of death, so there is always hope when we live life to the fullest. Seagulls struggle in a lonely battle against the wind and rain, and salmon persist upstream on a mission to spawn. They all strive until the very end. A lone boat in the storm still holds hope for rescue, and the wounded veterans of war sustain themselves with courage. When one is down in life, one should endeavor to turn over a new leaf, to stand up again, for courage and determination are the driving forces behind the will to live. Hope in life is not only sustained by courage, it is also sustained by vows and the wisdom to carry on. To live courageously is not to live for oneself only; it is also to live for one's family, for society, and for one's responsibilities. Only cowards shun life, while the courageous safeguard its existence.

In the face of hopelessness, we must maintain hope to the very end.

The Significance of Breathing

In the *Sutra of Forty-Two Sections*, the Buddha asked his disciples, "How long is one's life?" One of the monks replied, "A few years." The next one answered, "A few days!" Another one said, "Less than one day!" Another responded, "Between meals!" Finally, the Buddha said, "Life lasts for the duration of one breath."

Life is extraordinarily precious and yet it is based on a short breath, so breathing is extremely important to us. When there is sunshine, we do not recognize its importance, nor when there is a river, do we appreciate the value of a single drop of water. While we are still able to breathe, we never think about how precious and important a single breath is to us! However, once breathing ceases, wealth, status, fame, friends, and family all become meaningless.

Look at our senses: our eyes allow us to see, our ears hear, our arms and legs enable us to move, and our mouths allow us to talk. However, once breathing stops, our eyes, ears and body no longer function because our life exists on the strength of a breath. Though our eyes, ears, nose, mouth, and body all have their exclusive functions, only a breath can substitute for and even override all of them. Breath, unlike our eyes, cannot be used for seeing, but it can feel the differences in the atmosphere. Breathing is not used for hearing like our ears, but it can sense the anomaly in a relationship.

Breathing can feel the changes in the environment outside our body and also perceive the thought processes inside our mind. When we are relaxed and carefree, we can breathe easier, heaving a huge sigh of relief. Conversely, when we are under pressure, we may become short of breath. Breathing shows us life's versatility. It can sense if the air is fresh, and it can also observe the volatility of life. Therefore, looking after our breathing is protecting our lives.

Breathing can also be used for cultivation in adjusting one's life and purifying one's mind. In observing how we breathe in and out, we become aware of the condition of our body and mind. Rapid and short breathing signifies a flustered and unstable mind, and smooth breathing is indicative of a harmonized mind. Hence, the practice of counting breaths has always been emphasized repeatedly during meditation instruction.

Since we live in this world, we must cherish our breathing as we cherish our lives. When there still exists a single breath, we must make use of the opportunity to fulfill all our obligations, accomplish all our responsibilities and make good on all our promises. For any commitment we make to our country and community, parents and children, or friends and relatives, we must act appropriately and expediently. To build and strengthen our afinity with others, we should make prompt and good use of every single breath.

The Strength of Commitment

To "commit" is to give assurance to others and to make a conscientious effort to deliver a promise. To instill credibility and trustworthiness, we must honor our words. Confucius once said, "One without credibility is like a large vehicle without a brake pedal, or a small carriage without axles. How can one go anywhere?" Living up to one's word is a basic courtesy. In past agricultural societies, transportation was very inconvenient and modes of communication were underdeveloped. To deliver mail to and from home, people traveling on business relied heavily on couriers. But there was no contract between the parties, and there were rarely witnesses. There was only good faith. No matter how far the messengers needed to travel or how many obstacles they had to overcome, the deliveries had to be made. This is the strength of a commitment.

Ancient people took commitment very seriously. Many commonly used proverbs describe the value of commitment. Here are a few examples.

A promise is worth a thousand ounces of gold.
A promise is worth nine golden tripods.
Once one's words are spoken, they cannot be retrieved, even by four quick horses.
To befriend sincerely, one's word is one's faith.
If one's word proves one's faith, his actions are highly respected.

Politicians who keep promises gain the trust of voters, making it easier for them to enact legislation. Supervisors who adhere to their commitments inspire their subordinates, enhancing their confidence and faith. Friends who honor their word strengthen their friendships.

Some people not only make and keep commitments to people, they also make commitments of their time. For instance, Venerable Yi Jung and Venerable Shao Chueh of Fo Guang Shan have committed themselves to serve at the Lan Yang Senior Citizens Home in Ilan, Taiwan for thirty years. In honoring their pledge, they work diligently and never complain. As of today, they have yet to request a job change.

Some people make commitments, but with money. If they pledge a donation to assist others, they follow through with their promise. Some may make a commitment for the future, such as executing someone's will, or passing on a position or an office. Others are faithful in relationships. The numerous poems penned over the ages are testimony to the commitment couples make to love.

The ancients would commit a lifetime to honor a promise, readily sacrificing their lives if necessary. Unfortunately, people in modern society make casual pledges and break their word just as casually. So individuals are left with no choice but resort to written contracts, tape recordings, video tapings, witnesses, public notaries, trust funds, and other legal means to ensure that promises are kept. In dealing with others and handling affairs, one may gain temporarily by being crafty, but it is only by being trustworthy and realistic in our actions that we are able to really earn the lasting faith of others.

Strive for Progress Against All Odds

Adaptation and progress are laws of nature. Salmon push their way upstream to spawn, ensuring the survival of the species. Grass takes root out of harm's way to continue its growth. The branch of a withered flower refuses to die, despite the harsh conditions of winter. Therefore, when humans claim to be the most superior of all creatures, it would be very ironic if they lacked the skills of adaptation and the hearts of progress that other living organisms possess. It is human nature to strive for growth and advancement, for only water flows downstream.

Success, however, does not happen overnight or without effort. It is the result of endless struggle and hard work. It is to go against all odds for the attainment of something better. It is like a plum blossom that is full of fragrance in the cold of winter, or a lotus flower that blooms beautifully in the heat of summer. It is like those who work very hard to support their parents in spite of meager means. It is like those who persevere through years of study and hardship for a chance at fame and fortune. It is like the Buddhist teaching where, despite the fact that every living being is a potential bodhisattva with an inherent Buddha Nature, full enlightenment is possible only with diligent practice of the fifty-one stages of cultivation.

The United States, a world superpower, did not achieve her stature without a long struggle and the collective efforts of her people. Apartheid in South Africa did not come to an end without the courage and sacrifice of the racially segregated. In many parts of the world, people fight for religious freedom, political progress and social equality against all odds and at all costs. Be concerned with attaining an even higher level of cultivation - this is the wisest attitude to hold toward life.

To Be Unfettered by Worry and Joy

Our lives are neither worrisome nor joyful. We rejoice upon gains, although gains do not necessarily bring us joy. Similarly, to lose does not equal worry. Joy is not necessarily good and worry not necessarily bad. If your children rob or steal and then bring home stolen goods, it may appear initially that you are gaining a lot, but actually serious trouble is heading your way. Nowadays, people talk about being alert to the possibility of a crisis, for they realize that being able to bear short-term pain in the present can ensure peace in the future. So joy is not necessarily good, and worry is not simply adversity.

In order to be joyful, we should share our benefits with others, and not be envious of what others have, because selfless joy is the most valuable. Should we worry, it should be expressed as care for others and as concern for our cultivation. We should worry about chaos in society and the suffering of all sentient beings. There is nothing wrong with worrying about the problems of the world.

Joy is something everyone pursues, because it is more precious than fame and fortune. If you are rich and famous but live unhappily, life is meaningless. So there are those who find joy in frugality and the Dharma, others in freedom and ease, some in peace and harmony, and still others in contentment and serenity.

To feel worried and troubled is not necessarily bad either. If the Dharma is not propagated and sentient beings are not delivered, how could we not worry? We must recognize that real trouble occurs when a country is chaotic and human hearts are defiled. We should worry about the progress of our cultivation, our sincerity toward others, and about our ability to serve others well.

Worrying is the habit of a compassionate mind, and to worry about the Way and not about our own well-being is the realization of a compassionate mind.

There is an old Chinese saying, "One should not rejoice at material gains and should not lament for one's misfortunes. When one is in a high position, one should be mindful of his subjects, and when one is removed from power, one should have concern for his lord." We should not base our happiness on the suffering of others. We should not be joyful only about our own affairs, but instead we should be mindful of every living being in the world. Even as an average citizen, we should be joyful for the well-being and harmony of the entire family, for the cooperation and neighborliness of the community, and for the welfare of our superiors. All in all, we should feel joy for the happiness of others.

Joy brightens the world with colors and fills our lives with hope. If there is only worry and joylessness, then we will not be able to understand life. To be meaningful, life should be filled with both joy and worry. But to be unfettered by joy and worry is to attain an even higher level of cultivation, which would be the wisest attitude to hold toward life.

To be unfettered by joy and worry is to attain an even higher level of cultivation.

To Live in Hope

The worst tragedy in life is to live without hope for the future. When there is hope, there is a future. One of the mottoes of the Buddha's Light International Association is "to give others hope." That is the highest act of benevolence. On the other hand, to disappoint and render others hopeless is the cruelest act.

People live in hope. Parents raise their children with hope for the future. They teach and educate their children so the children will have hope for their own futures. We get along with our neighbors so there is hope for everyone to live in harmony. We plant trees and grow flowers; we save up for a rainy day. There is endless hope in life. The Chinese place great emphasis on passing things down from generation to generation, a sentiment to sustain their lineage. Nowadays, organ transplants offer hope for the perpetuation of life.

For a country, people pay taxes in the hope that the nation will be better established; the government builds highways and bridges in the hope that transportation will improve. We conduct charity work in the hope of advancing social welfare; we elect capable leaders in the hope of promoting democracy; and we penalize offending officials in the hope of creating a more honest government. We hope for a mild climate, prosperity and world peace. All of these constitute our hopes for the future.

Those who recite the Buddha's name hope to be reborn in the Pure Land, and those who are Christian hope to go to heaven. We do good deeds and give to others in this life in the hope that we will do better in our next. We plant and cultivate this year in the hope that we will have a bumper crop in the next. We all hope to enhance our moral values, benefit others with our compassion, and improve our ability to understand and reason.

When we have hope, we have a future. We need not fear darkness, for we know that dawn comes after the darkest hour, and that there will be hope. We need not dread the ice and snow of winter for soon enough spring will arrive with fresh hope. We need not worry when we are strapped for cash, for even with only a single dollar, there is hope for us to make a fortune.

Life is only meaningful when we have hope. People often give up on themselves because they lose hope. When faced with setbacks and misfortune, if we are willing to change the conditions and to take initiative in helping others, the light of hope can be re-lit. Those who are ready to give up their lives when all hope seems lost should bear in mind, "Upon the death of a life of selfishness is born the second life of benevolence." They should be able to turn a new leaf and start a second life. Many cancer patients get involved in social service and rekindle their light of life in the process of their own healing. If people have self-confidence and pledge to serve others, the brightness of their lives will not only illuminate others but also ignite the light within their own hearts.

It is Chinese tradition to wish each other the best on birthdays, when moving to a new home, on anniversaries, and at the New Year, congratulating and blessing one another with hope for the future. In life we come and go; in time we have this year and the next. If we can have hope all the time, then we will enjoy endless opportunities, and we will truly live in hope everyday.

Walk the Right Path

There is a saying that goes, "Life is like a traveler." On the path of life, everyone has his or her own path. The *Awakening of Faith in the Mahayana (Mahayana Sraddhoptoda Sastra)* explains that "one mind has two gates," one is the "gate of thusness" and the other is the "gate of life and death." They represent the two paths of life, the right path and the wrong path. Only your wisdom can help you decide which path to choose!

The paths in this world include broad and smooth ones, as well as narrow and rugged ones. When you walk on the broad path, your way is easy and smooth, and you can charge ahead with few obstacles. But if you take the narrow path, your passage is rough and blocked by obstructions, and you find it difficult to travel. Our feet can become a part of our path, as can our mouths. We only need to ask for it. Our hands can help create the path of our future, and our minds can build for us the path to a wonderful life.

The paths in life are either material or formless. Our career paths can be in different professions, and our spiritual paths can lie in different religions, skills, knowledge, and interests. Our future paths could be in heaven or hell, as hungry ghosts or as animals. Some strive arduously to travel a smooth path in life, but some scheme deviously and find themselves going down a path of no return. Then there are insidious people, people without moral values, who end up on the long path of darkness.

So where is our path in life? Though our path here is only a brief journey in the eternity of life, all of us should endeavor to walk the right path. What is the right path? As children, the right path is to practice filial piety and honor our parents. As husbands and wives, the right path is to love and respect one other. As students, the right path is to work diligently in school. As friends, it is to help and look after each other. All these are our paths in life.

Those in business would like to profit from their capital, those in government would like to contribute to their country and citizens, those in the armed forces would like to guard their homeland, and those in religion would like to uphold right views and right thoughts. These are all right paths to take, and we should never digress from them.

Confucianism teaches, "It is better to be lacking but right than it is to be affluent and deviant." In order to be successful in our endeavor, we should always be candid, giving others joy and doing things to benefit others. But nowadays there are unethical developers who build unsafe houses and endanger the lives of others. There are immoral lawyers who create trouble by initiating unnecessary lawsuits just to make a profit. There are also shrewd bankers who scheme and manipulate to earn a dollar. Unfortunately, these people only know how to be deceitful. They do not take the right path but go down a deviant one instead. In the end, they will reap the bitter fruit of their own errant designs.

The sutra teaches, "Bodhisattvas fear causes and sentient beings fear effects." The right path is a sure way to reach heaven, and the deviant road is the one to hell. Which path would you like to take?

Where There is Dharma, There is a Way

When the public loses hope and becomes skeptical about life due to social problems, violence and lack of moral values, the saying, "where there is Dharma, there is a way" is something we can all reflect upon. It is indeed a refreshing breeze in the inferno of defilements, renewing our faith and hope in life.

We all hope for prosperity, a good reputation, career success, and harmonious relationships with others so that we can establish a fulfilling life. Actually, to enjoy a good reputation, we just need to be truthful and speak well of others. In order to achieve wealth, we need to practice generosity and give to others. Bill Gates, of Microsoft, is not only the richest man in the world, he is also the top philanthropist in America because of the generous donations he has made.

Within families, there are always problems with relationships because of the changing dynamics between the sexes. But if spouses would observe the precept of no sexual misconduct, support each other with kind words and amity, and strive to uphold their love, then harmony in the family can be attained.

For a nation to be stable and affluent, its leader should govern wisely and be mindful of the needs of the people. In Indian history, King Asoka was well known for his conquests on the battlefield. He successfully annexed all the neighboring states, but he governed with an iron rule and failed to win the hearts of his subjects. After he converted to Buddhism, however, he awakened from his delusion and changed his errant ways. Thereafter, he ruled ethically and with compassion, and his good reputation won him a place in history as one of the greatest monarchs. This triumph of Buddhism over force is beyond all comparison.

Although many people admire the law and order of Western countries, little do they realize that these nations respect and practice the spirit of the law. In Austria, newspaper boxes are simply hung on utility poles, and people put money in the box to purchase a newspaper. No one takes them for free, and nobody steals money from the box. The Austrians demonstrate to us that the precept "do not steal" is the best law indeed.

Unfortunately, the world is still filled with perversity and darkness. But we should pledge to purify the prevailing social ills with Buddhism. In practicing Buddhism, right views can help us all unlock the benevolent and bright side of our nature. Truly, where there is Dharma, there is a way.

A Moment of Awakening

On New Year's Eve, 1999, people all over the world anxiously awaited the dawn of the new millennium. As the sun appeared on the horizon, their excitement could no longer be contained. Their emotions reached a new climax, and their spirits were lifted by the promise of the first light.

Desire and worry trouble many of us in this world. Our minds are polluted by our surroundings. We have become anxious and fearful, without a moment of peace and clarity. All around us, there are people who choose to stay in their own private hell by clinging on to their worries. There are those who have imprisoned their minds with egotistical attachments. And there are others who choose to become slaves of material possessions. It really does not matter what we have decided to do with our lives and minds because, in the middle of the night, when all is quiet, each and every one of us will long for a moment of awakening.

We will long for a moment when we can exile all of our hatred, desires and jealousy - a moment devoid of ignorance and defilement. In the middle of the night, we reflect on what we have done and wish for a chance for true freedom. A moment of awakening is of immense value. It is the root of goodness. According to the Buddhist texts, "A mind of purity outweighs all of the world's gold; wisdom and enlightenment are a part of every living being." It is that moment of awakening that allows sages to be at ease with their surroundings and leaders to listen to good advice. It is that moment of awakening that allows wrongdoers to repent their transgressions and murderers to have a change of heart. Without that moment of awakening, good conditions will not come about, and we will live in eternal darkness.

When bad desires arise in our mind, we should not worry too much. Instead, we should fear being ignorant of their existence. Only in a moment of awakening will we be able to see through the dark clouds and find the light of hope. Only in a moment of awakening will our minds have clarity and be freed of all defilements. Only in a moment of awakening will darkness be dispelled and our minds enlightened.

In this world of impermanence, let us ignite the inner light of awakening; let us rediscover our innate wisdom in this time of turbulence; let us sow the seeds of compassion in times of hatred and learn to forgive our enemy; let us foster the power of confidence when faced with doubts and illuminate the light of wisdom in times of darkness; let us have hope in despair and find solace amidst sorrow. We must eradicate all of our doubts, confusion and selfishness, for compassion comes from kindness, truth from clarity, and the beauty of human nature from a moment of awakening.

A moment of awakening is of immense value.

Freedom from Fear

Disasters, calamities and accidents are common natural disasters that occur throughout the world. Everyday we live amidst danger and fear, afraid of what will happen to us next. Walking down the street, we might get stabbed because we accidentally bump into the wrong person or look in the wrong direction. Driving down the freeway, we might be assaulted by an attacker. Even in the mall, our purse could mysteriously disappear while we are trying on a new pair of shoes. No matter where we are, danger awaits us. Fear has become a part of our lives.

After a devastating earthquake that topples concrete buildings, we question the safety and durability of our homes. After a killer hurricane that sweeps across our hometown and causes massive landslides, we begin to wonder how many times we have to endure such destruction.

We are also vulnerable to man-made calamities. Drive-by shootings and environmental pollution have become everyday headlines in the newspaper. No matter where we are, it seems there is no escape from danger and fear. Everywhere we turn, we are exposed to harm and risk. Since the early 1980's, we have lived in the shadows of AIDS, and the situation has yet to show sign of improvement. It is still a worldwide epidemic, despite advances in medical research. The "3 in 1" cocktail, a new AIDS treatment, can only delay the onset of the disease; it is not the cure that everyone has been hoping for. Therefore, AIDS remains the Black Death of the twentieth century.

In recent years, an increasing number of computer users have taken advantage of the unlimited resources on the Internet. More and more people have logged on to the various chat rooms available on the worldwide web. At the same time, unfortunately, more and more perverts have used the Internet to distribute child pornography and lure children away from the security of their homes. Nowadays, parents have to worry when their children turn on the computer to surf the net. They are worried whenever their young ones are out of sight. The world has changed, and our homes are no longer exempt from unwanted intrusions and danger.

Even when the U.S. economy prospered and the unemployment rate was at an all-time low, people still worried about inflation and the rise of interest rates. At the slightest hint of an economic slow down, investors panic and the stock market suffers dramatic changes. In everyday life, it seems like the world is full of bad news.

When we turn on the television or read the morning paper, all we hear and see are reports of foul play and destruction. Murder, air pollution, ethnic cleansing, war in third world countries, natural disasters, and other negative stories have made us more and more apprehensive of the world in which we live. Thus, we anxiously wait for the moment when everyone will be free from danger and fear, the moment when everyone will enjoy everlasting peace and security.

In order to attain that goal of freedom from peril and apprehension, steps must be taken by the authorities, as well as by ordinary citizens. The government must enact laws that will guarantee justice, equality and happiness for all. It must always take into consideration the interests and well-being of the people and pass legislation that will ensure personal and public safety. Individual rights and freedom must be respected at all times, including the right to a life without fear and danger. However, to be truly free from worry and harm, as individuals, we must purify our minds and elevate our moral standards by means of religious beliefs and practice. Only when we are truly free in our minds can we live in a world without danger and fear.

We can purify our minds through religious beliefs and practice.

To Forbear a Moment's Anger

"To bear disgrace and insult" is the most important virtue a person can possibly cultivate, because the ability to forbear is enormously powerful, since a moment of anger can destroy an entire lifetime of merits. By restraining our emotions, we have a better chance of avoiding confrontation and gaining control of the situation at hand. Otherwise, our minds will be clouded and our judgment impaired. We must understand that in forbearance, we have an opportunity for greater achievement, because if we cannot forbear in small matters, how can we be destined for great undertakings?

In today's society, people often mistake "forbearance" for "cowardice." Therefore, the inability or unwillingness to forbear anger has become a source of social and family violence. All too often we have seen a simple quarrel turn into a major gunfight, or a plain argument into a regrettable tragedy. Spousal abuse, child abuse and drive-by shootings result from the inability of people to control their emotions. If people can withhold their anger for even a moment and let their emotions settle, they would reap unimaginable benefits. If people could see the merit in forbearance, tragedy and personal losses would be minimized. Therefore, if we want to have peace and order in our lives, reason must prevail over negative emotions.

What does it mean to "forbear?" It is not very difficult for most of us to endure a moment of hunger or thirst. It is not very hard for most of us to bear the heat of summer or the cold of winter. However, it is very difficult for most of us to forbear anger. Even great men and women of history have succumbed to such a fate. By losing control of their emotions, many lost their ability to perceive things clearly and made irreversible mistakes that changed the course of history and profoundly impacted the lives of many generations. Therefore, the decision to forbear or not to forbear is a determining factor in one's ultimate success or failure. If we wish to be successful in our undertakings, we must learn to hold back our emotions and be as thoughtful as possible in our actions and reactions.

"To forbear" is indeed an act of courage and not a symbol of cowardice. It takes great effort and resolution to endure pain and hardship. It requires tremendous confidence to bear insult and disgrace without a hint of retaliation or self-doubt. In today's society, our willingness to tolerate and accept those who are different from us will not only promote social harmony, it will also help to prevent needless tragedy.

In order for us to practice the virtue of forbearance, we must have strength, wisdom and compassion. We must be willing to settle differences or disputes by means of reason and kindness. We must believe in tolerance and restraint as signs of goodness and bravery. Therefore, if we want to succeed in life and bring about a more peaceful world, we must learn to control our emotions and not to be affected by a moment of anger.

What does it mean to "forbear"?

To Purposely Confuse the Bad with the Good

According to the Buddha's teachings, good phenomena are occurrences that are beneficial and bad phenomena are those that are harmful. When people ignorantly choose the bad over the good, their lives will be miserable and unsatisfactory because they insist on attempting to satisfy their desire with more craving or are unwilling to appreciate what they already have. We often see the rich spend lavishly on luxury, or the powerful use their position to bully the poor. We often see people indulge in elaborate meals or adulterous behavior, instead of reverting to a simpler way of life. Worse yet, people seem to purposely confuse the bad with the good in order to achieve their goals. It should come as no surprise, then, that the world is full of chaos and disorder.

In order for us to rectify the situation, we must learn to differentiate the good from the bad and choose the former over the latter. We must learn to not intentionally misconstrue the bad as something good. There should be no excuse for misbehavior and no justification for wrongdoing. A crime is a crime, regardless of the cause or condition. Just take a moment to imagine a world in which kidnapping is excusable as a lesson to the wealthy, and murdering one's wife is a means to peace and quiet; a world in which killing one's newborn baby is an acceptable way to a carefree life, and distributing child pornography over the Internet is a method for learning to use a computer. We must ask ourselves if we really want to live in this kind of world, a world in which the wrong and the bad can be justified as something good and right. If we want our lives to be free of crime and confusion, the answer should and must be "no."

Since it is no mystery that human beings are not perfect

and mistakes are unavoidable, we must learn to feel regret and shame for our missteps. We must take responsibility for whatever harm we cause. Instead of running away or trying to make excuses, we must accept the consequences of our misbehavior. Instead of intentionally confounding the wrong with the good, we must admit to our mistakes and vow to try our best to avoid them in the future. If we learn to have a strong sense of guilt, the wrong can be corrected and then eradicated. A feeling of embarrassment, disgrace or unworthiness should be the driving force behind our efforts to prevent the bad from happening and to refrain from wrongdoing.

Therefore, if we want to restore order to society, we must shun the bad and the wrong. We cannot permit anyone to use excuses to justify or accept what is bad as good. We cannot allow ourselves to offer a reasonable justification for transposing the bad with the good. We must see wrong actions as wrong and right actions as right and accept no alternative. We cannot grant any exception, regardless of the situation, lest a floodgate open and anarchy prevail.

We must see wrong actions as wrong and right actions as right - and accept no alternative.

To Have Resolve and Make Vows

When athletes race, they need a finish line; when archers compete, they need a target. In the journey of life, we need similar goals in order for us to progress with assurance.

To have resolve and to make vows means that we must establish a target for ourselves. As children we all have our ambitions and goals. We may have dreamt of becoming a scientist, an educator, engineer, pilot, or a doctor. These dreams are resolutions. However, after we grow up, how many of us realize these dreams? One of the reasons we may not could be that we develop new goals in life. However, for most people, it is due to a vow that lacks support and strength. Without the motivation to progress, we are unable to persevere in our ideals, and, in the middle of our pursuit, we easily give up.

Having resolve and making vows is like filling a car with gasoline or winding up a clock, making ready to forge ahead in full motion. Conversely, if we do not have a goal or a direction, then we are like a boat without a compass. How can we sail to the other shore on the wide, open sea without a compass? There are some who wish to pay homage to Manjusri Bodhisattva at Mount Wutai, but they never take any action. Two, three or even more years pass, with only empty words. How will they ever complete the pilgrimage?

To have resolve and to make vows is the motivation behind our becoming saints and sages. In Buddhism, the Buddhas and Bodhisattvas all make great vows on their path of practice, such as the forty-eight great vows of Amitabha Buddha, the twelve great vows of the Medicine Buddha, the ten great vows of Samantabhadra Bodhisattva, and the twelve compassionate vows of Avalokitesvara Bodhisattva. The vows of the Buddhas and bodhisattvas are like the timetables students set for completing assignments. When we have goals and motivation, then we can progress step by step on our paths and realize our ideals.

In the past, many sages and heroes realized great achievements because of their resolve and vows, just as Venerable Master Xuanzang made a vow to propagate Buddhism, and brought back many volumes of the Buddhist teachings from India to China. Therefore, we all need to have resolve and make vows in life so that we have motivation to persist. In today's society, we especially need people to have resolve and to make vows. Policemen need resolve to carry out their duty to rid society of crime and violence, to correct its errant ways, and to bring peace to the community. Homemakers should resolve to practice filial piety, to teach their children well, to look after the family, and to enhance its joy and harmony. Students must resolve to do well in their studies, to respect their parents and teachers and to excel in both academics and ethics. Every one of us should resolve to give others joy and to share with others whatever good we have so that there is peace and harmony in society.

To make a vow is like mining an energy source; for inside us is a mine filled with endless energy and limitless treasure. It is only when each of us has resolve and makes vows that we are able to write our own history and the legacy of our family, to leave behind compassion for society and light for the world. What kind of resolve and vows would you like to leave behind?

Avalokitesvara Bodhisattva is known by most Buddhists because of his compassionate vows and actions.

The Truth is the Path

There is a saying, "Aspiration is not deterred by old age, and the truth is not enhanced by verbosity." Truth is the equilibrium in relationships between people, matter and nature. There are many reasonable people in this world and many who are not. We all need to realize that with the truth we can go places, and without it we cannot go anywhere. Therefore, we must have truth when dealing with others and in handling our affairs. Then, we can have anything we need and go anywhere we want to go.

Some of us may have the truth, but because of selfishness and ignorance, we lose it. On the other hand, some people do not have the truth, but if they are humble and admit their faults, they may instead gain it. There are many who are wealthy and others who are learned, but those who understand the truth are few in number.

Confucius said, " If one understands the truth in the morning, one can die the same evening." Eventually, money can all be spent, but the truth can last more than a lifetime. Since ancient times, the sages have taught us to understand the truth. Those who fail to understand the truth do so mostly because of their selfishness and the greed and jealousy bred by it. Naturally, they cannot understand it.

Confucianism teaches, "The Way can be practiced only when the world is shared by all." Because the world is shared and enjoyed by all, it is not the private property of any single group or family. This is also the highest ideal of the founder of modern China, Dr. Sun Yat-sen. As we have often witnessed in countries throughout the world, governments usually fail if they are controlled solely by a single person who overrides the wishes of the ruling party or even the country. Rulers who ignore public opinion and pass legislation contrary to the wishes of the citizens are often abandoned by their countrymen.

In reality, a nation is the assembly of its citizens, so governments and rulers are not superior, because the country belongs to its citizens. Only when a country and its citizenry share all can the way of truth be achieved. But how many can truly appreciate the essence of this?

Truth is the equilibrium in relationships between people, matter and nature.

The Value of Truth

Truth is the highest guiding principle in the universe and in life. All phenomena are guided by their own principles, including heaven and earth, humans and matter, and sense and emotion. But all principles need to be in accordance with the truth, not contrary to it. So what is truth? Truth is in conformity with the principle of cause and effect. As the saying goes, "When one plants a melon seed, one gets melons, and when one plants a bean, one harvests beans." Another way to say it is, "Good begets good and evil begets evil." This principle is applicable to everything in the universe.

The religions of the world all claim to be the truth. There seems to be truth everywhere, so what is truly in accordance with truth? Truth can only be proven over time, space and among people. Truth must be universal, equal, inherent, and enduring. For example, as humans, we all must die. This holds true for both men and women, throughout history and the entire world. Therefore, the impermanence of life is truth.

Truth is also in accordance with the principle of cause and effect, for that is the fairest judge of our universe. While "fairness" does not seem to exist in the world, it is only in Buddhism that we can truly see what is fair. We need to understand this. Wrong cannot obscure reason; reason cannot overcome the law. Law cannot overpower authority; authority cannot defeat the universal truth. Universal truth is the principle of cause and effect, the highest law.

Truth is not limited only to religion. Truth permeates the universe and every corner of the world. In Buddhism we say, "A universe exists in a flower and a Buddha is found in a leaf." The world of nature expresses the truth of life, be it the summer streams or the autumn valleys, the blossoms of spring or the snows of winter. We need only to pay attention and to listen with our minds. Then, we can hear truth in the gushing brooks as they cascade over the rocks.

Seeking truth is the noblest hope of humans, and spreading truth their noblest mission in life. Truth is in accord with nature. When we are at ease, we are in accordance with nature. When we are carefree, we live in accordance with truth. Conversely, when we work against the truth, we are doomed to fail.

Truth is a priceless treasure to which even gold and silver cannot compare! How many of us really know what truth is? We see politicians rally for votes before an election, but if they fail to serve the public every day, how can they possibly win the support of the voters? If we do not plant seeds in spring, how can there be a harvest by fall? If we never seek affinities with others when we are doing well, how can we expect others to help us when we are in trouble? Some may commit all sorts of evil deeds, and when their acts catch up with them, they blame everyone but themselves. We often say that heaven is always watching us. Heaven is the principle of cause and effect, for everything is guided by truth. Therefore, we should always take the right path in all we do. That is the path to truth.

One flower, one World; one Leaf, one Tathagartha.

The Meaning of Compassion

Although "compassion is the foundation of Buddhism" is a popular slogan, compassion is not the exclusive property of Buddhists. It is a common treasure shared by all sentient beings. Because there is compassion in this world, life is full of meaning. As we endure the trials and tribulations life offers us, compassion inspires us with endless visions.

The mind of compassion is the ever-flowing fountainhead of all living things, because compassion is Buddha Nature. Sentient beings can attain Buddhahood because of compassion. Compassion is also the basic quality of being human, for one can be without everything but still have compassion! When we have compassion, our speech and actions are like sunshine, pristine water, or a pretty flower, bringing light, purity and joy to the world.

Compassion is not just offering sympathy. If we stand up to fight for truth and justice where there is oppression or for the righteous when they are slandered and attacked, then we are acting courageously and practicing real compassion. The practice of compassion requires wisdom because it is not simply a kind thought; it is helping others by being wise and reasonable. Compassion is not just going along with the crowd, but serving others by holding the right views and thoughts. It is neither attempting to selfishly benefit one's own friends and family, nor currying favors. The highest level of compassion should be completely selfless and equal for all.

Compassion is the actual practice of our ethics, not the standard by which we measure others. It is not limited to only providing kind words of praise and encouragement. Sometimes circumstances may require us to exercise forcefulness in order to prevail over atrocities that are being committed. This is more difficult, but nevertheless a practice of great compassion. In today's society, many people often misinterpret the meaning of compassion and let forgiveness and magnanimity be reduced to leniency and indulgence, disrupting social order in the process. Compassion is sometimes misused in a degenerative manner that may even result in or encourage crime. For example, randomly freeing live animals might result in their death; giving away money arbitrarily might foster greed. Therefore, the practice of compassion must be directed by wisdom; otherwise well-meaning intentions can be completely ruined.

Compassion should not be static but rather a continuous sublimation of care and good will. The *Flower Ornament Scripture (Avatamsaka Sutra)* says, "One only wishes for the liberation of all sentient beings from suffering, but does not hope for one's own serenity." True compassion, then, lies in the willingness to be burdened by the concerns of the world and also to be delighted by the happiness of all humanity. There are many unfulfilled dreams in this world, and when we practice compassion, we sometimes come up short ourselves. However, only compassion can restore peace and harmony amidst conflict; only compassion can create the affinity needed to succeed in any endeavor. Compassion is truly the inexhaustible treasure of life!

Ksitigarbha Bodhisattva vows that he will not achieve Buddhahood until he has liberated all beings from hell.

Follow the Circumstances

Living in today's complex society, how can we maintain our correct views of right and wrong, undistracted by those with unwholesome practices, and yet be able to get along well with others? The *Awakening of Faith in the Mahayana (Mahayana Sraddhotpada Sastra)* teaches us "to follow circumstances without changing our principles."

To follow circumstances means that we should follow causes and conditions, because all phenomena in this world arise out of the joining of causes and conditions. All living organisms live under the principle of causes and conditions. The thoughts and actions of one person have an effect on the causes and conditions of the next person. Therefore, in getting along with others, we should follow beneficial causes and conditions, because it is always better to build positive connections with others than to create grudges. To be able to follow circumstances helps us accomplish our goals.

To follow circumstances is to follow the conditions that present themselves, and not to act randomly or casually. In addition to being able to follow circumstances, we also need to remain "unchanged" in our principles. Following circumstances without changing our principles is the best prescription for benefiting the self and others. During the Tang Dynasty, a popular princess "followed circumstances" and married a Tibetan prince in order to foster the relationship between China and Tibet. By becoming an ambassador of peace for her motherland, not only did she bring Buddhism to Tibet, she also brought the culture of the Tang Dynasty to her adopted home. Her achievements are still remembered and lauded by many today. On the other hand, there are also many cases in history in which a kingdom was lost and its ruler killed because those in power failed to "follow circumstances."

We must understand that to "follow circumstances" does not simply mean to conform to trends and follow along with anything that arises; to remain "unchanged" does not mean we blindly follow tradition and refuse to change. In society many people follow circumstances but lose their principles and sense of value. They follow trends and, in the end, become mired in suffering, unable to free themselves. Others are too persistent with their principles and fail to integrate with the circumstances around them. Their attachments not only sever positive connections with others, they also obstruct the progress of their work.

Therefore, we can be in control of our lives if we live according to the circumstances and maintain our principles and values at the same time. Those in high places should always be aware that their thinking and the policies they implement affect the development of the nation and the welfare of its residents. Therefore, it is imperative that they always be open to ideas and consult with capable people for advice. They should also be perceptive of current conditions and follow the circumstances before them. They should never shut themselves off from advice in the belief that traditional practice is the best way, under any circumstance. In the end they harm themselves as well as others and may even earn themselves positions of infamy in the history books. In this respect, should we not be cautious?

The tree is able to follow their circumstances to grow, and they beautify the world.

Levels of Faith

From birth to adulthood, from childhood to maturity, in the various stages of life every person at one point or another has someone he or she admires or idolizes. During early childhood, children have complete trust in their parents and believe their every word without doubt. Once they start school, their teachers become their idols and role models. It seems that no matter what the teacher says, the teacher is always right because the teacher knows it all.

Depending on upbringing, education and social background, each of us develops a different perspective and sense of value. Hence, there are people who believe that money is almighty; whereas others hold romance as superior; some consider friendship as their top priority; still others deem freedom as the most invaluable; and some devote themselves entirely to religion. Belief is spontaneous and comes from within our inner nature. However, belief is not necessarily the same as religion. For instance, some people immerse themselves in a kind of idealism or philosophy, while others idolize or revere a particular person; these beliefs may or may not be connected to a form of religion.

Nevertheless, when we question issues of life and death, we always turn to religion. People are religious beings in need of beliefs. Religion is like light, and humans cannot live without light. Religion is like water, and humans cannot survive without water. From pre-historic times, prior to the development of any knowledge, humans have always believed in nature. What ensued is their faith in supernatural powers, deities and eventually in the sovereignty of their rulers. Over time, beliefs have progressed to include democracy, human rights and even the rights of the unborn. In short, since the beginning of civilization, other than the pursuit of material comforts, humans have always sought to sublimate themselves to spiritual life and religious beliefs.

When it comes to religion, though, we must exercise extreme caution, for if we follow unorthodox or cult-like teachings it can be like taking poison. Usually, it is too late when we realize our mistake because our lives could already be in great peril. Therefore, it may be better not to believe in any religion rather than to believe in a cult. However, it is better to have blind faith than not to believe in any religion at all. Blind faith is based on fear of the unknow; the problem is a lack of understanding, because the concepts of cause and effect and good versus evil do exist. As for people who do not believe in anything, they are like those who do not think, or those who close their eyes to the world: they never come to understand what the world is really like.

Of course, the best choice we can make is to believe in a religion that is righteous! The Buddhist teachings of the middle path, dependent origination, the principle of cause and effect, on birth and death, and on nirvana can help people resolve the questions of life. However, even for Buddhists, there are different levels of faith. Some believe in people rather than the Dharma; others believe in the temple instead of the religion; still others believe in relationships and not in the teachings; while some believe in deities rather than in the Buddha.

Furthermore, there are also different levels of belief in the teachings of Buddhism. The prajna, or wisdom, at the laity level is right view; the prajna of the Arhat is dependent origination; and the prajna of the bodhisattva is emptiness. Only the Buddha is able to truly attain prajna, for that is the level of the Buddha. In reality, "prajna" is our inner Buddha Nature, and the main reason for us to learn Buddhism is to develop and actualize our inner Buddha Nature. So in learning Buddhism, we should begin by praying to and worshipping the Buddha, and progress to learning from, practicing and actually becoming the Buddha. It is only when we become a Buddha that we have reached the highest level of faith.

To elevate our level of belief is very important.

True Equality

Once a cat caught a mouse, and as he was about to eat it, the mouse protested, "Both you and I have a life. We should be equal. Why do you want to eat me?" Upon hearing that, the cat realized that the mouse knew what equality is and demanded it. He replied, "OK, then you can eat me instead." The mouse asked, "You are a cat and you're so much bigger than me. How could I possibly eat you?" The cat shot back, "You're so small. Since you cannot eat me, then I'm going to eat you." The mouse was dumbfounded! Then the cat said, "You don't need to fight anymore. This is actually quite equal!"

Equality is not achieved by subduing others by means of force. It should be achieved by treating others as you would like to be treated, and trying to put yourself in their shoes. Equality means caring for the self-respect and basic rights of others, for it is only when there is mutual respect that the self and others can truly be equal.

The Buddha said, "When rivers enter the ocean, they are no longer called rivers; when the four castes become monastics, they share the same Sakya name." Buddhism advocates that, "everyone possesses a Buddha Nature." This equality in self-nature is true equality. Theoretically, Buddha and sentient beings are equal; however, phenomenologically there is a difference due to cause and effect. When viewed from the standpoint of self-nature, everyone can attain Buddhahood; but in reality, because the causes and conditions and the merits of individuals are not the same, there is differentiation between saints and commoners. Therefore, "in the nature of equality, sentient beings and the Buddha do not exist even in name; and in the realm of thusness, self and others do not have a form." This is also equality.

Children sometimes demand to be equal to their parents and question why their parents are seated at the head of the table. If children demand to be on the same footing as their parents, they are being ignorant of ethics and equality, because equality means having an order for the young and the aged. A subordinate who demands to be equal to his or her seniors thinks, "If the seniors are equal, then why aren't I equal to them?" Similar to the first case, a person who demands to be treated the same as his or her seniors is ignorant of customs and equality, because equality also means differentiation according to seniority and rank.

True equality means having an equal starting point for all, but not all necessarily being equal. In a race, the starting point for each athlete is the same, but when the starting signal sounds off and everyone charges ahead, the speed of individuals vary. Each person tries his or her best to win, and it would be impossible to demand that everyone arrive at the finish line at the same time. This is true equality.

Fishermen make their living from the sea, which we often take for granted. When mountaineers hunt for birds, they are harshly criticized for their actions in the name of protecting migrant birds. So does that mean birds should be protected while beings in the sea should be food for men? Whenever there are natural disasters, such as earthquakes and floods, all walks of life in the community join together to lend a helping hand to the victims. This is equality for the moment; however, what society needs is even more equality every day, at ordinary moments.

Advocating equality can help eradicate the inequalities in the world and should be founded on mutual respect for self and others. It means not distinguishing between large and small or rich and poor, for all should be respected before equality can be achieved. When the self and others, sentient beings and the Buddha, nature and phenomena are all equal, then there will be peace in the world.

To Reform Oneself

When a table is broken, it needs to be fixed; when a shirt is torn, it needs to be mended; when the roof is leaking, it needs to be patched; and when a road is wrecked, it needs to be repaired. Similarly, we need to change and transform ourselves continuously. In order to achieve eventual perfection we need to work on correcting our bad habits.

Confucius once said, "Man is not born with knowledge, knowledge is gained by learning." There is so much to learn that it is impossible to learn it all in a lifetime. So if we feel too satisfied with ourselves and refuse to reform ourselves or to continue to learn, then we never improve. We are full of bad habits. In speech, we have harsh speech, meaningless speech, duplicity and lies; and in thoughts we have selfishness, attachments, greed, anger and jealousy. These are like cancer, for if we fail to find a good doctor and proper treatment, it is like being marooned onboard a sinking ship. Life becomes precarious and helpless! It is only when we are able to reform ourselves and find our own cure that we are able to find hope.

Throughout history there are many examples of people who changed their delinquent ways and errant practices, reforming their lives from being the outlaws of their time to becoming the saints of their era. During the Buddha's time, there was a notorious murderer, Angulimalya, who after learning the devious teachings of some heretics killed mercilessly. But after he met the Buddha, who compassionately taught him the right way, he transformed himself completely and eventually became an Arhat who was pure in body and mind.

Nagarjuna is one of the four renowned Buddhist shastra

masters in ancient India. Before he learned Buddhism, he lived a life full of sin, spending his days flirting with the ladies of the imperial palace. But upon learning Mahayana Buddhism, he submerged himself completely in the Dharma. He eventually became the patriarch of the eight schools of Buddhism and is now honored as a Bodhisattva.

The large bell in the Buddha Hall once protested to the statue of the Buddha, "Why do the devotees all come to worship you but hit me hard instead?" The statue of the Buddha replied, "That is because I withstood the carving and hammering of the chisel and mallet, so I could become a statue for people to worship. But you wail loudly whenever you are struck, so you can only be a big bell!"

Whether we become a statue of the Buddha for people to worship or a big bell that cannot stand to be struck depends on whether or not we are willing to reform ourselves. One sutra says, "Everyone has Buddha Nature; Buddha Nature is intrinsically pure." Therefore, even if we have erred, as long as we are able to purify our karma and cease to commit further misdeeds, we should be able to turn over a new leaf. Furthermore, we should consistently review and reform ourselves so that greed can be turned to generosity, anger to compassion, ignorance to wisdom, and jealousy to respect.

In regard to daily life, we should practice "see no evil, hear no evil, speak no evil, and do no evil." When we can be rid of our bad habits, subdue and control the six roots, the eyes, ears, nose, tongue, body and mind, then life will be free of wrongdoing.

Patience and Persistence

Influenced by today's "instant culture," modern people tend to expect instant results in anything they do. Practitioners want to have attainment in this life, scholars want to become instant laureates in their fields, and entrepreneurs want to gain a huge fortune overnight.

As the saying goes, "A flower picked before its time is not fragrant, and a fruit so picked is not sweet." Regardless of what we set out to do, without deep cultivation and planning, and long-term nurturing and development, nothing can be done well. The twigs from a one-year-old tree can only be used for firewood, wood from a ten-year-old tree can be used for chairs, but only the timber from a hundred-year-old tree can be used for beams and pillars. Before rice is fully cooked, we should not open the pot, and before an egg is properly hatched, we should not crack the shell. Being able to pass the test of time, and being patient and persistent are the foundations of success.

Being patient is an art, and being persistent is a kind of hope. Having patience and persistence can help us understand what we study, achieve in our practice, and appreciate life. There are numerous examples of ancient scholars who easily spent a decade studying for just one national examination and persisted in their endeavors until they achieved success. Renowned calligrapher Wang Xizhi practiced his calligraphy by a pond, using tank after tank of water for ink, and over time became one of the few calligraphy masters in Chinese history.

It is only when we are patient and persistent that we are able to plant deep roots; with deep roots, we are then able to grow thick branches and lush leaves. In this world, as long as we are willing to learn patiently, anything can be accomplished. The world-famous carvings in Tunhwang of Kansu Province are the wondrous creation of thousands of artists over the dynasties who spent their lives expressing their wisdom in artwork. If it were not for the patience and persistence of the generations of artists, we would not be able to see such brilliant art today.

The importance of patience and persistence to the success of any endeavor cannot be emphasized enough. However, impatience seems to be a common ill among today's younger generation. The lack of persistence is also revealed in the callousness of today's youth. It seems that young people do not possess the patience and concentration required for stability in life. Being physically and mentally unsteady, they change jobs often, and, lacking in perseverance, they cannot settle down in their careers or in a company. How then is it possible for their employers or supervisors to entrust them with responsibility? Without the trust of their superiors, how are they going to succeed?

If a rolling stone gathers no moss, how is it possible for a moving rock to become the cornerstone of an enterprise? We should often ask ourselves, "Am I patient in my studies, my work, and in dealing with others?" If we lack patience and persistence, then it is like digging a well and giving up just short of its completion. How could we drink the water? Therefore, the secret to success is simply cultivating patience and persistence.

Only the trees with deep roots can grow thick branches and lush leaves.

Humility and Shame

The most exquisite piece of clothing in this world is not made of pearls or feathers, nor is it made of silk or mink. It is the "attire of humility and shame." Humility and shame are the most beautiful clothes and the best kind of cosmetics. If we know how to be humble and feel ashamed of our shortcomings, we will naturally emanate an air of nobility and auspiciousness. A Buddhist sutra states, "The attire of humility and shame is auspicious beyond compare."

Humility is being concerned about the transgressions we commit against others through our unwholesome actions or thoughts, the ensuing shame we feel for these transgressions, and how we repent for and correct them. With humility and shame, we can become motivated to improve and progress. There are numerous examples in Chinese history in which those who were ashamed of their plight were motivated to accomplish great success.

A thought of shame, and reflection upon our actions, can result in the sublimation of our character into a nobler and purer nature. "If our conscience is always clear towards the heavens and our behavior does not transgress upon others," then we are almost perfect in our morals and practice. On the other hand, people who are shameless and without humility, with their consciences deluded by greed, anger and jealousy, will engage in all sorts of vicious acts and lose their humanity. A person without humanity is like a tree without bark. How is a barkless tree going to bear fruit?

Nowadays many people feel victimized and complain that their country does not look after their welfare or that their friends and relatives do not care for them. Have they ever reflected upon how much they have contributed to their country or what kind of care they have provided to those around them? If they review themselves conscientiously and attempt to understand the protection their country provides them, the nurturing of parents, the guidance of teachers, the care of family, and support of friends, then they will feel truly grateful and humbled. How can they possibly complain?

Confucianism teaches, "To be shameful is akin to courage." When we possess a thought of shame, there also exists a thought of goodness. One should not fear being incapable, nor having made mistakes, but instead should fear being pessimistic and self-defeating, giving up on oneself. There once was a brilliant student who was reprimanded in public by his teacher for being untidy. If he had reflected on his shortcoming, he would surely have advanced in his schoolwork. However, he just gave up on himself and regressed in his studies. Perhaps teachers should also re-evaluate their way of teaching, especially in being mindful of students' self-respect and discipline.

Those with humility and shame are able to correct their behavior and move ahead. They are able to develop sound morals and positive actions. If each person can cultivate humility and shame, be shameful of his or her ignorance, lack of morals, and inadequacies, and can incorporate humility and shame into his or her behavior and thoughts, then, be it in speech or in silence, in action or in rest, we can all enhance our ethics and gain great benefits.

Vanity and Practicality

As the saying goes, "An exterior of gold and jade belies an interior of rot and decay." Many young people today only care for external appearance and not for practicality. There is a joke that clearly illustrates how totally meaningless and valueless vanity is.

Two people were arguing and bickering with one another, unable to settle their differences. Gradually, a crowd of vain people gathered around them, looking for a way to break them up. First, someone with a mouthful of golden teeth went up to them and said, "Stop your arguing. Let me give you a bright smile!" And in saying so, he smiled broadly, displaying his mouthful of shiny gold teeth.

Then someone with a powdered face got up quickly and pointed to his face saying, "Please don't fight anymore! Just give me 'face'!"

Another person wearing a large gold ring on his finger came forward, swinging a clenched fist in the air and declared, "If you two carry on any longer, I'll punch you both!"

Then a person wearing new shoes moved to the front and proclaimed, "If you want to keep arguing, I'm going to kick you!" And in so saying, he lifted his trouser leg and raised his foot to kick.

Finally, a person wearing new clothes rushed up and shouted loudly, "Please don't argue any more! I will bear what it takes!" And he patted his chest in saying so.

This group of vain people could not persuade anyone with their reasoning, nor were they able to win anyone over with their morals. They only wanted to show off what they were wearing, unaware that greatness cannot be displayed through appearance and apparel. These days many people insist on buying only designer-brand items and clothing that they like to show off. They crave the praise of others and are often boastful of themselves. Such impracticalities are the display of a vain mind.

We should have both feet on the ground in whatever we do, and, should we decide to undertake any endeavor, we should strive for the long-term and not for the moment. There are many examples throughout Chinese history in which kings and heroes persevered for years before they reached their goals, and scholars who spent a decade preparing for an examination. Through their examples, we learn how success can be achieved through hard work and practicality.

Conversely, if we are vain and unrealistic in what we set out to do, we are like a tree without roots. A tree without roots easily withers, like a building with a poor foundation that is liable to collapse at anytime. We should be fully aware that vanity is only for the moment, but practicality lasts over time. Just as Venerable Master Xuanzang once said, "One should speak not of fame or fortune, but should act with practicality." That is the best exemplar for us to follow.

If the tree is without roots, it will wither easily.

Having and Using

Everybody wants to have, but the problem in having lies in discontent. After eating a full meal, one craves gourmet cuisine; after marrying a wonderful wife, one longs for a pretty mistress; after owning a house, one hopes for a mansion; after securing a job, one yearns for a higher position; and after earning thousands, one pursues millions. Our precious life is spent in the pursuit of 'having,' and we in the course of doing so become duly troubled.

So what are the standards of having? The wealthy have so much property, land, jewelry and stocks, but they are often fearful and may be unable to sleep well at night. Compared to a scholar who is content and happy with his lot, willing to shoulder the responsibility of the world and always mindful of all sentient beings, who actually has more? As the Chinese saying goes, "One may own ten thousand acres of fertile land, but how much food does one consume a day? One may own a thousand mansions, but how much space does one take to sleep at night?"

To have wealth and property but fail to use it is the same as not having, thus rendering it useless. A river should flow so it can provide water to all, and air should move about so it can bring life to everyone. Therefore, in accordance with the law of nature, when we make a fortune from the community, we need to spend it on the community. Instead of striving to have, one should advocate using. The first step in using is to give. Edison demonstrated a higher level of using by applying his inventions to improving the welfare of humankind. Bill Gates demonstrates a high level of 'using' by donating his profits to benefit needy school children and society. However, it is not easy to use our resources properly, for once we are attached to wealth and property as belonging to the 'self,' then those we intend to benefit are fewer. Our attitudes and methods in using would become incorrect and inappropriate.

We come into this world empty-handed, and we will leave in the same manner. Our wealth and property are also realized from nothing, and should therefore be given away similarly. Regarding everything in the world, would it not be wonderful if we could maintain emptiness and be able to use all we have in reality? There is a saying in Buddhism, "We own the whole universe in our minds and embrace endless realms in our hearts." To have is limited and measurable, but to be empty is limitless and immeasurable.

If we are mindful of using, we can relate to the truth, and if we use our wealth, we can resolve the world's troubles. So let the narrowness of selfish-having be replaced by the having of causes and conditions and the having of togetherness. Let the deviance of possessiveness be obliterated by the having of appreciation and gratitude. Therefore, having is wealth but using is wisdom, and to have both wealth and wisdom would be real benevolence.

Who can own the ocean?

Begin From the Self

Once a young student and his friend went hiking. On the way the student became weary and stopped to rest. His friend reminded him, "I can do anything for you, but I can't eat or sleep for you." The young student replied, "I know how to eat and sleep. You don't need to do that for me." His friend said, "It's the same with walking, I can't do it for you."

A devotee asked a Chan Master how to become enlightened. The Chan Master got up and left. After he took a few steps he turned around and said, "I'm going to the bathroom. Can you do that for me?"

The above stories are quite simple but profound in meaning because they illustrate that in whatever we do we must rely on ourselves. We need to begin from the self in order to achieve anything. The widow who loses her husband must wipe away her tears so she has the strength to raise her children. Children who lose their parents must strive on so they have the courage to face reality. Helen Keller beat all odds and shared her achievements with the world. She did not give up but instead embraced life with optimism and involved herself in the world around her, benefiting herself as well as others. She set an exemplary standard for relying upon oneself as the key to the road of success.

When young birds learn how to fly, the mother bird does not let them return to the old nest. In Western society, when children reach their legal age, they are expected to move away from home. Even though teachers guide and instruct their students, students still need to be diligent in order to find the key of knowledge. We may have friends to help us, but if we do not make affinities, how are others going to help us?

Mountains collapse and people grow old; neither should be relied upon. If we do not begin from the self, but only seek external help, even if we have relatives in high and powerful places, they are only able to provide relief momentarily. Many people only know how to ask for favors but do not know how to sow and cultivate. What will they harvest?

We must help ourselves before others can render us help; we must respect ourselves before others will pay us respect. We are the cause and others are the condition. Avalokitesvara Bodhisattva holds a string of beads used to recite Avalokitesvara Bodhisattva's name in order to show us that we should rely on ourselves. In Chan practice, both the practitioner and the teacher work together to achieve enlightenment. Chan Master Huangbo once said, "Do not be attached to the Buddha, do not be attached to the Dharma and do not be attached to the Sangha." It is only when we begin from the self and cultivate diligently that we can then taste the sweet fruits of success.

When the young bird learns how to fly, the mother bird does not let it return to the old nest.

Be Optimistic and Progressive

There are numerous types of people in the world and just as many kinds of personalities. Some are lackadaisical and listless while others are optimistic and progressive. Those who are lackadaisical and listless live in idleness and believe that there is nothing much worth doing in life. They are full of complaints, thinking the whole world has let them down, creating worries and frustrations for themselves as if they live only to suffer. It is regrettable that they choose to live that way.

On the other hand, those who are optimistic and progressive are eager to move on in life. Filled with hope for the future, they are full of energy. They are open-minded and tolerant, ready to take on any responsibility, and consider everyone they come across as representing good causes and conditions. Not only do they live a joyous life, they also share the fragrance of happiness with others.

We should not start out by blaming others for how they treat us. Instead we should first consider our own personalities. If we are active in improving ourselves, passionate about work, and courageous and enterprising, then naturally we appreciate the true meaning of life. But if we are close-minded, full of grudges, and bogged down with worries and frustration, then it is difficult for us to compete with others in any undertaking.

A good illustration of optimism and progressiveness is Confucius himself, who was so much engaged in his learning and teaching that he did not realize he was aging. He was, "Too diligent in his studies to take a meal and too happy with his work to be worried." Prince Bhadra was a cousin and also a disciple of the Buddha. In his practice of Buddhism, he lived in the mountains, wearing only simple clothing and carrying an alms bowl. Although he took only one meal a day, he was filled with Dharma joy. Even President Clinton made plans for his future upon his retirement from the presidency. We saw him doing chores in the television documentary about his daily life, doing his own laundry and cleaning the floor of his home. He is open-minded, optimistic and progressive, so he is able to be at ease and plan for his new life.

To be optimistic is not just for the enjoyment of oneself, but rather it is for the benefit of others. Those who are optimistic do not blame others for small matters, just as many Chan masters in the past lived joyous and carefree lives in their practice, while bringing happiness and ease to those around them at the same time. People who are optimistic always fare better than those below them, while those who are pessimistic are frustrated that they are not as good as those above them. Optimism is like a light shining on a future filled with hope, and pessimism is like a narcotic eroding the well being of the spirit. To be optimistic and progressive enables us to live a joyous life and to realize the hope and confidence of life.

Each of us enjoys the use of twenty-four hours every day. Some spend the hours seeking pleasure, their decadent lifestyles leading them nowhere. Others use their time to serve others, their fulfilling lives truly meaningful. Both types of people spend the same amount of time, but the outcomes are vastly different. So the cultivation of an optimistic and progressive view is something we should not overlook in life.

People who are pessimistic are frustrated that they are not as good as those above them.

Twelve Questions for Introspection

In order to advance good merit and elevate our moral character, we must constantly ask ourselves the following twelve questions as a means of introspection and reflection:

1. Since I am a member of human society, what have I done to benefit my fellow human beings?
2. Have I tried my best to repay the generosity and kindness of my parents and teachers?
3. Have I returned the many favors that others have bestowed upon me?
4. Have I done anything to bring harm to my parents, family, friends, teachers or society?
5. Since others have provided me with good causes and conditions in areas of daily necessities, have I done the same for them?
6. Do I truly understand the meaning of rebirth?
7. Have I taken a good look at myself and counted how many times a day I have traveled to hell and back?
8. Can I explain how my actions and thoughts have revolved around greed, hatred, ignorance, and jealousy?
9. In self-examination, what are the first three things that I reflect upon?
10. How can I attain a life of true happiness without attachments?
11. How can I eradicate defilement, worries and ignorance to rediscover my Buddha Nature?
12. How can I plan my life so I can have good causes and conditions here and now?

It is clear that the twelve questions were designed to help us improve ourselves in the area of interpersonal relationships, because in today's society, egoism prevails over altruism, and self-interest takes precedence over the welfare of others. There are simply too many people nowadays who have placed their own interest above that of the country and society, which has led to all kinds of corruption and social illness. Instead of examining their own thoughts and actions, they choose to blame others for their own pitfalls. Some even go so far as to blame fate for their misfortune. What they fail to realize is that the real problem lies within them. Their misery and suffering are caused by their ignorance of what is truly right and wrong.

Sixth Patriarch Huineng once said, "By having a good lot without a good heart, one's good fortune will be short-lived; by having a good heart without a good lot, one's life will be well provided for; by having neither a good heart nor a good lot, one's life will be impoverished forever." In Buddhism, there are many examples of those who were not endowed with talent, but attained enlightenment with hard work, and there are those who were born with a silver spoon in their mouths, but have wasted away their good fortune with selfish acts and intentions. For example, Devadatta, cousin of the Buddha, selfishly attempted to murder the Buddha and destroy the

While seeing the flower, have you experienced the Dharma?

Sangha. Therefore, we must be careful of our actions and intentions, because we will reap the fruits of what we sow. No matter how advanced science and technology may be, we must first demand the most of ourselves and strengthen our moral character for the sake of survival in this world of chaos.

We must be introspective and reflect upon our actions and volition in order to cultivate good causes and conditions for the betterment of our lives. By constantly asking ourselves "The Twelve Questions of Life," we will be able to elevate ourselves to a higher level of fulfillment.

The Definition of Success

In this world, there are those who succeed easily in their careers, and there are others who are good at nothing. Just as some who excel academically and become renowned scholars, others spend their lives getting nowhere in their undertakings. Farmers who harvest a bumper crop are successful in their cultivation, and workers who achieve high production are also successful at their jobs. In today's democratic elections, winning the election means success, and losing means failure. In the past, many people successfully built their enterprises, but some could only help others to succeed. As the saying goes, "The success of a general in the battlefield is based on the bones of thousands." Success is therefore often based on the strength of many.

Some find it hard to succeed in anything they do and fail easily in whatever they attempt. This may be ascribed to poor timing as well as to having insufficient causes and conditions. Then there are those who appear to be successful but are actually failures, and others who seem to have failed but can be considered a success overall. There are many cases in history in which unscrupulous rulers succeeded in taking control of a country, only to be deemed failures in the history books. There were others who lost power or even became captives of the enemies, yet they were lauded for their integrity. Genghis Khan was a fierce conqueror and succeeded in his conquests of many countries, but his ruthlessness only earned him the fear of his subjects. Former President Richard Nixon was successful in enhancing the international status of America through his foreign policies, but the Watergate scandal brought him great infamy in history.

The line between success and failure is indeed very fine.

Those who succeed may breed arrogance, and those who are arrogant are doomed to fail. But those who fail and do not cease in their efforts are the ones who reap the final fruit of success. In this world, we may fail in our finances, our careers, or in love, but if we succeed as a human, then we are successful in life.

The definition of success is not based on social status, material wealth, academic achievement, or physical attributes. Rather, it is judged on the scales of conscience and moral values. Some give up their lives for a righteous cause. Do you regard them as failures? Others own billions of dollars in personal assets, but are despised by everyone. Do you consider them to be successful? Therefore, success and failure are not absolute, for the most important standard lies in whether or not conscience and moral judgment exist within us.

Farmers who harvest a bumper crop are successful in their cultivation.

Trust and Reputation

The ancients said, "A man cannot establish himself without trust." The Chinese character for the word "trust" is made up of the two characters "human" and "speech," meaning if one's speech is not trustworthy, then one is not worthy of being human. Conversely, if we are trustworthy and keep our word, then we can surely gain the trust of others, as well as a good reputation.

Trust is the moral that connects all worldly ethics, for one who is trustworthy is also someone who is credible. Trust and credibility are the foundations of all enterprise, a traditional Chinese virtue, for conduct that is contrary to trust and credibility is considered a major character flaw. We can easily be tested in everyday life to see if we are trustworthy; for example, our punctuality, the sincerity of our speech, and the strength of our promises can all be tested.

Trust is the promise one agrees to keep, and it should last an entire lifetime. Buddhism teaches "no false speech," which means to be trustworthy. Those who are trustworthy do not speak empty or meaningless words, but instead keep their promises. As the saying goes, "Once the words of the wise are spoken, even the fastest horse cannot retrieve them." Furthermore, in order to be considered trustworthy, one should not forge, infringe on copyrights, commit perjury, cheat, embezzle or own possessions illicitly. For those who keep their word, their promise is better than the word of law. But those who are untrustworthy might even break a binding contract after it is signed.

Trust is a milestone on the path of success; in business, trust is an intangible asset and, in cherishing it, great profit can be gained in addition to helping others to succeed at the same time.

Trust smoothes out dealings in business and in family matters, be it between spouses, parents and children, or even between lovers, friends, coworkers, or countries. It should never be forfeited in the face of profit. In Chinese history there are many examples of kings and generals who were willing to give up great material gain to keep a promise, and thereby won themselves a good reputation and trust. But in today's world, many nations easily break the promises made to each other. Though in politics neither friends nor enemies last forever, for the realization of world peace there should be trust between countries.

Trust is wealth and "a promise is worth a thousand pieces of gold." Money lost can be regained, but a ruined reputation is irreplaceable. Therefore, from personal dealings with others to global peace, trust should never be jeopardized or lost. Without trust, how can we establish ourselves in the world? We all should beware!

Glossory

Amitahba Buddha: *The Buddha of Infinite Light or Infinite Life. Amitahba is one of the most popular Buddhas in Mahayana Buddhism. He presides over the Western Pure Land.*

Amitahba Sutra: *The Amitahba Sutra is one of the three sutras that form the doctrinal basis for the Pure Land School of Mahayana Buddhism.*

Angulimalya: *While under a teacher of Brahmanism in Sravasti, Angulimalya was instructed to kill and cut off the fingers of a hundred people. This act, he was told, would complete his practice. Consequently, Angulimalya killed ninety-nine people and, because it was against his nature, he went mad. He was about to kill his own mother when, fortunately, he met the Buddha and converted to Buddhism. Angulimalya repented of his evil ways and jointed the Sangha.*

Asanga: *He founded the Yogacara School of Buddhism, along with his brother, Vasubandhu. He lived in the fourth century C.E.*

Asoka: *He reigned as the King of the Maurya Kingdom in India from 272-236 B.C.E. He was the foremost royal patron of Buddhism in India and the first monarch to rule over a united India.*

Avalokitesvara Bodhisattva: *Literally, "He who hears the sounds of the world." In Mahayana Buddhism, Avalokitesvara is known as the Bodhisattva of Compassion. He can manifest himself in any* *form necessary in order to help any being. He is considered one of the great bodhisattvas in Mahayana Buddhism.*

Avatamsaka Sutra: *Translated in English as The Flower Ornament Scriptures; in Chinese, Huayan Jing. It is one of the major texts in Mahayana Buddhism. This sutra is the first teaching expounded by the Buddha after his enlightenment.*

Bodhisattva: *"Enlightening being." Anyone who seeks Buddhahood and vows to liberate all sentient beings.*

Buddha: *"Awakened one." When "the Buddha" is used, it usually refers to the historical Buddha, Sakyamuni Buddha.*

Buddhahood: *The attainment and expression that characterizes a Buddha. Buddhahood is the goal of all beings.*

Buddha's Light International Association (B.L.I.A.): *A worldwide Buddhist organization dedicated to the propagation of Humanistic Buddhism, founded by Master Hsing Yun in 1992. Today, B.L.I.A. has over one million members.*

Buddhist Canon: *The Buddhist teachings known as the "Tripitaka" or "The Three Baskets." They are divided into three categories, the sutras (teachings of the Buddha), the vinayas (precepts and rules), and the Abhidharma (commentary on the Buddha's teachings).*

Cause and Condition: *Referring to the primary cause (cause) and the secondary causes (conditions). The seed out of which a plant* *or a flower grows is a good illustration of the primary cause; the element of soil, humidity, sunlight, and so forth, could be considered the secondary causes.*

Cause and Effect: *The most basic doctrine in Buddhism, which explains the formation of all relations and connections in this world.*

Chan: *The form of the Chinese transliteration of the Sanskrit term, dhyana; it refers to meditative concentration.*

China's Cultural Revolution: *A comprehensive reform movement in China, which was initiated by Miao Zedong in 1965 to eliminate counter revolutionary influences in the country's institution.*

Confucianism: *The philosophy named after Confucius. It was the official philosophy of China, established in the third century B.C.E.*

Confucius: *(551-479 B.C.E) In Chinese, "Kung Tzu." He was an early Chinese moral philosopher.*

Cultivation: *Synonymous with "practice." Cultivation is the training of heart and mind in generosity, virtue, calmness, wisdom, etc.*

Dadian: *(732-824 C.E.) Also known as Dadian Baotong, he was a Chan Master of the Tang Dynasty.*

Daosheng: *(355-434 C.E.) A Buddhist scholar of the Nirvana Sutra in the Chinese Eastern Jin Dynasty. He claims that non-sen-*

tient beings can also attain Buddhahood.

Dependent Origination: *A fundamental Buddhist doctrine, which teaches that all beings and phenomena exist or occur because of their relationship with other beings or phenomena. Therefore, nothing can exist in absolute independence of other things or arise of its own accord.*

Dharma: *With a capital "D": 1) the ultimate truth, and 2) the teachings of the Buddha. When the Dharma is applied or practiced in life, it is 3) righteousness or virtues. With a lowercase "d": 4) anything that can be thought of, experienced, or named; close to "phenomena."*

Diamond Sutra: *The Vajracchedika Prajna Paramita Sutra. The Diamond Sutra sets forth the doctrine of emptiness and the perfection of wisdom. It is named such because the perfection of wisdom cuts delusion like a diamond.*

Eight Winds: *The conditions that hinder people from remaining faithful to the right path. They are prosperity, decline, disgrace, honor, praise, censure, suffering, and pleasure.*

Emptiness: *Skt. "sunyata." A fundamental Buddhist concept, also known as non-substantiality or relativity, meaning all phenomena have no fixed or independent nature. In Buddhism, it can be divided into two categories: 1) Associated with individuals and called "non-substantiality of persons." 2) Associated with phenomena and called "non-substantiality of dharmas." Therefore, the concept of emptiness is related to dependent origination and impermanence.*

Fifty-two stages of cultivation: *Referring to the Fifty-two Levels of the bodhisattva path. A detailed analysis is presented in the Avatamsaka Sutra.*

Five Aggregates: *"Five Skandhas." They represent the composition of body and mind. The Five skandhas are form, feeling, perception, mental formations, and consciousness.*

Five Precepts: *The five basic moral precepts of Buddhism. They are no killing, no stealing, no lying, no sexual misconduct, and no intoxicants.*

Gongan: *A word, sentence, or "case study" used as a tool for cultivation in Chan Buddhism.*

Han Yu: *(768-824 C.E.) An eminent literary figure who took it upon himself to weaken the influence of Buddhism in order to restore Confucianism.*

Heart Sutra: *One of the most important sutras in Mahayana Buddhism. It is regarded as the essence of Buddhist teachings and is chanted daily in communities all over the world.*

Huineng: *(638-713 C.E.) A very influential Chan Master. Huineng was the Sixth Patriarch of the Chinese Chan lineage.*

Impermanence: *One of the fundamental truths taught by the Buddha: everything arises and passes. Nothing is constant, even for a single moment.*

Karma: *This means, "work, action, or deeds" and is related to the law of cause and effect. All deeds, whether good or bad, produce effects. The effects may be experienced instantly or they may not come into fruition for many years or even many lifetimes.*

Ksitigarbha Bodhisattva: *One of the great Bodhisattvas of Mahayana Buddhism. Ksitigarbha Bodhisattva vowed to remain in hell until all sentient beings are released from it.*

Kuan Yin: *(Guanyin): Also known as Avalokitesvara in Sanskrit.*

Linji: *(? - 867 C.E.) Also known as Linji Yixuan, he was a famous Chinese Chan Master of the Chinese Tang Dynasty. He was also the founder of Linji School of Buddhism.*

Linji Chan School: *"Rinzai" School in Japanese. It is one of the Chinese Chan Schools.*

Lotus Sutra: *This sutra is one of the most important sutras in Mahayana Buddhism. The major emphasis in this sutra is the concept of integration of the vehicles of the sravakas, pratyeka-buddha's, and bodhisattvas.*

Mahayana: *Literally, "Great Vehicle." One of the two main traditions of Buddhism, Theravada being the other one. Mahayana Buddhism stresses that helping other sentient beings to achieve enlightenment is as important as self-liberation.*

Mahayana Sraddhotpada Sastra: *From Sanskrit, it is translated as Treatise on the Awakening of Faith in Mahayana. The*

Awakening of Faith is a commentary on Mahayana Buddhism. It explains basic concepts of the teachings and is used particularly in China as an introduction to Mahayana.

Medicine Buddha: *In Sanskrit, "Bhaisajyaguru." The Buddha of Healing. He presides over the Eastern Pure Land. In previous lives, when he practiced the Bodhisattva Path, he made twelve great vows to help sentient beings eliminate the suffering of physical and mental illness and to guide them towards liberation.*

Merit: *The blessings of wealth, health, intelligence, etc., which are accrued by benefiting others and by practicing what is good.*

Middle Way: *A teaching of Sakyamuni Buddha, which teaches the avoidance of all extremes.*

Mount Wutai: *Literally, "Five-Terrace Mountains." It is one of the four most famous mountains in China. It is a very important pilgrimage site for Chinese Buddhists who venerate the Bodhisattva Manjusri (Wenshu).*

Nagarjuna: *Born in Southern India in the second-third century. He is the founder of the Madhyamika School (the Middle School) and the author of many commentaries and treaties. His famous works include Treatise on the Perfection of Great Wisdom, Treatise on the Middle Path, the Merits of Right Deeds Sutra, and many more. Therefore, he was given the title of "Master of a Thousand Commentaries." He is a very important philosopher in Buddhism.*

Nanjing Massacre: *In July 1937, Japan launched its full-scale invasion of China, leading up to what is now considered one of the worst systematic massacres of civilians and crimes against humanity.*

Nirvana: *Pali, "nibbana." The original meaning of this word is "extinguished, calmed, quieted, tamed, or dead." In Buddhism, it refers to the absolute extinction of individual existence, or of all afflictions and desires; it is the state of liberation, beyond birth and death. It is also the final goal in Buddhism.*

Parinirvana: *A synonym for "nirvana." It is the state of having completed all merits and perfections and eliminated all unwholesomeness. Usually, it is used to refer to the time when the Buddha physically passed away.*

Patriarch: *In Buddhism, a patriarch is the founder of a school and the successors in the transmission of the teaching.*

Prajna: *Literally, "wisdom." Prajna is the highest form of wisdom. It is the wisdom of insight into the true nature of all phenomena.*

Pure Land: *Another term for a Buddha realm, which is established by the vows and cultivation of one who has achieved enlightenment.*

Sage: *In this context, sage refers to arhats, bodhisattvas, or Buddhas.*

Sakya: *The tribe in ancient Northern India, which Sakyamuni Buddha belonged to when he was Prince Siddhartha.*

Samantabhadra: *The Bodhisattva of universal goodness. He personifies transcendental practices and vows. He is usually depicted riding a white, six-tusked elephant, which symbolizes the six perfections.*

Sangha: *The Buddhist community, including both monastics and laypersons.*

Sentient Being: *Any living being that has a consciousness.*

Sastra: *A commentary or treatise on Buddhist sutras.*

Six Realms: *The various modes of existence in which rebirth occurs, ranging from the lower realms of hell, hungry ghost, and animal to the higher realms of human, asura, and heaven.*

Supernatural Power: *That which is beyond or above the natural or cannot be explained by natural law.*

Sutra: *The scriptures directly taught by the Buddha.*

Sutra of Forty-Two Sections: *The first sutra translated into Chinese, completed by Kasyapamatanga and Zhu falan. The content is concise and explains the basic doctrines of early Buddhism. The emphases are on the explanations of the fruits of monastic attainment, the karmas of wholesomeness and unwholesomeness, the awakening of the mind, the abandonment of desires, the concept of impermanence, and the important meaning of becoming a monastic and of learning the path.*

Ten Directions: *In Buddhism, this term is used to refer to* *everywhere, indicating the eight points of the compass (north, west, east, south, southeast, southwest, northeast and northwest) plus the zenith and nadir.*

Three Realms: *The realm of desire, the realm of form, and the realm of formlessness.*

Vasubandhu: *(320-380 C.E.) He founded the Yogacara School of Buddhism, along with his brother, Asanga.*

Western Pure Land: *The realm where Amitabha Buddha presides. It came into existence due to Amitahba Buddha's forty-eight great vows. Sentient beings can make a vow to be reborn there where they can practice without obstructions until they attain enlightenment.*

Xuanzang: *(602 -664 C.E.) A great master in the Chinese Tang Dynasty. He is one of four great translators in Buddhist history. He studied in India for seventeen years and was responsible for bringing many collections of works, images, pictures, as well as one hundred and fifty relics to China from India. His famous work is entitled Buddhist Records of the Western Regions.*

Yosemite National Park: *A national park in California in the Sierra Nevada mountain range area.*

Yunmen: *(864-949 C.E.) Also known as Yunmen Wenyan. He was the founder of the Yunmen sect in the Chinese Chan School.*

Zhaozhou: *(778-897 C.E.) Also called Zhaozhou Congren. He was a Chan Master in the Chinese Tang Dynasty. He is famous for composing many koans (gongans).*

About Venerable Master Hsing Yun

Venerable Master Hsing Yun was born in Jiangdu, Jiangsu province, China, in 1927. Tonsured under Venerable Master Zhikai at age twelve, he became a novice monk at Qixia Vinaya School and Jiaoshan Buddhist College. He was fully ordained in 1941, and is the 48th Patriarch of the Linji (Rinzai) Chan school.

He went to Taiwan in 1949 where he undertook to revitalizing Chinese Mahayana Buddhism on the island with a range of activities novel for its time. In 1967, he founded the Fo Guang Shan (Buddha's Light Mountain) Buddhist Order, and had since established more than a hundred temples in Taiwan and on every continent worldwide. Hsi Lai Temple, the United States Headquarters, was built outside Los Angeles in 1988.

At present , there are nearly two thousand monks and nuns in the Fo Guang Shan Buddhist Order. The organization also oversees sixteen Buddhist colleges; five publishing houses including, Buddha's Light Publishing, Hsi Lai University Press; four universities, one of which is Hsi Lai University in Los Angeles; a secondary school; a satellite television station; an orphanage; and a nursing home for the elderly.

A prolific writer and an inspiring speaker, Master Hsing Yun has written many books on Buddhist sutras and a wide spectrum of topics over the past five decades. Most of his speeches and lectures were compiled into essays defining Humanistic Buddhism and outlining its practice. Some of his writings and lectures are translated into different languages, such as English, Spanish, German, Russian, Japanese, Korean, etc.

The Venerable Master is also the founder of Buddha's Light International Association, a worldwide organization of lay Buddhists dedicated to the propagation of Buddhism, with over 130 chapters and more than a million in membership.

About Buddha's Light Publishing and Fo Guang Shan International Translation Center

In 2001, Buddha's Light Publishing was established to publish Buddhist books translated by Fo Guang Shan International Translation Center as well as other valuable Buddhist works. Buddha's Light publishing is committed to building bridges between East and West, Buddhist communities, and cultures. All proceeds from our book sales support Buddhist propagation efforts.

As long as Venerable Master Hsing Yun has been a Buddhist monk, he has had a strong belief that books and other documentations of the Buddha's teachings is the way to unite us emotionally, help practice Buddhism at a higher altitude, and continuously define as well as challenge our views on living our lives.

In 1996, the Fo Guang Shan International Translation Center was established with this goal in mind. This marked the beginning of a string of publications translated into various languages from the Master's original writings in Chinese. Presently, several translation centers have been set up worldwide. Centers in Los Angeles and San Diego, USA; Sydney, Australia; Berlin, Germany; Argentina; South Africa; and Japan; coordinate translation or publication projects.

English Publication by Venerable Master Hsing Yun

Buddha's Light Publishing:
1. Between Ignorance and Enlightenment (I)
2. Between Ignorance and Enlightenment(II)
3. The Awakening Life
4. Fo Guang Study
5. Sutra of the Medicine Buddha
   - with an Introduction, Comments and Prayer
6. From the Four Noble Truths to the Four Universal Vows
   - An Integration of the Mahayana and Theravada Schools
7. On Buddhist Democracy, Freedom and Equality
8. Of Benefit to Oneself and Others
   - A Critique of the Six Perfections

Wisdom Publications:
9. Only a Great Rain
   - A Guide to Chinese Buddhist Meditation
10. Describing the Indescribable
    - A Commentary on the Diamond Sutra

Weatherhill, Inc.:
11. Being Good
    - Buddhist Ethics for Everday Life
12. Lotus in a Stream
    - Basic Buddhism for Beginners

iUniverse.com, Inc.:
13. Humble Table, Wise Fare
    - Gift for Life

Peter Lang Publishing:
14. The Lion's Roar

Hsi Lai University Press:
15. Handing Down the Light
16. Perfectly Willing
17. Happily Ever After
18. How I Practice Humanistic Buddhism
19. Where is Your Buddha Nature
20. The Carefree Life
21. Humble Table, Wise Fare
    - Hospitality for the Heart (I)
22. Humble Table, Wise Fare
    - Hospitality for the Heart (II)
23. Cloud and Water
    - An Interpretation of Chan Poems
24. Contemporary Thoughts on Humanistic Buddhism

Fogung Cultural Enterprise Co., Ltd.
25. Where There is Dharma,
    There is a Way
26. The Everlasting Light:
    Dharma Thoughts of Master Hsing Yun

Photo Credits:

Venerable Yi Chao	Page 7, 23, 25, 44, 54, 75, 83, 100, 103, 124
Venerable Miao Jie	Page 4, 17, 58, 68, 86, 88, 90, 98
Venerable Chueh Sheng	Page 19, 115, 121
Pi Lai	Page 1, 28, 30, 38, 50, 64, 66, 94, 117
Mei-Chi Shih	Page 13, 21, 92, 96, 119
Mu-Tzen Hsu	Page 42, 44, 48, 109
Betty Li	Page 113

Notes

Notes

Notes

Notes